Show and Tell Writing: From Labels to Pattern Books

Lucy Calkins, Series Editor
Marie Mounteer and Lizzie Hetzer

Photography by Peter Cunningham
Illustrations by Kimberly Fox and Marjorie Martinelli

HEINEMANN ◆ PORTSMOUTH, NH

To my mom, Debbie, and my dad, George—for being my first, and best, audience.
—Lizzie

To my parents, John and Rena—who taught me how to never give up.—Marie

Heinemann
361 Hanover Street
Portsmouth, NH 03801–3912
www.heinemann.com

Offices and agents throughout the world

© 2018 by Lucy Calkins, Marie Mounteer, and Lizzie Hetzer

All rights reserved. No part of this book may be reproduced in any form or by any electronic or mechanical means, including information storage and retrieval systems, without permission in writing from the publisher, except by a reviewer, who may quote brief passages in a review, with the exception of reproducible pages, which are identified by the *Show and Tell Writing: From Labels to Pattern Books* copyright line and can be photocopied for classroom use only.

> *The authors have dedicated a great deal of time and effort to writing the content of this book, and their written expression is protected by copyright law. We respectfully ask that you do not adapt, reuse, or copy anything on third-party (whether for-profit or not-for-profit) lesson-sharing websites. As always, we're happy to answer any questions you may have.*
>
> **—Heinemann Publishers**

"Dedicated to Teachers" is a trademark of Greenwood Publishing Group, Inc.

The authors and publisher wish to thank those who have generously given permission to reprint borrowed material:

From *The Ultimate Book of Vehicles,* by Anne-Sophie Baumann and Didier Balicevic (Twirl/Chronicle Books, 2014). Used by permission of Groupe Bayard.

From LIFT THE FLAP TAB: ON THE GO © 2014 by Roger Priddy. Reprinted by permission from Macmillan Publishing Group, LLC d/b/a St. Martin's Press. All rights reserved.

From *The Zoo*, by Rose Lewis. Courtesy of Pioneer Valley Books.

Cataloging-in-Publication data is on file with the Library of Congress.

ISBN-13: 978-0-325-10580-2

Editorial: Karen Kawaguchi
Production: Elizabeth Valway and Abigail Heim
Cover and interior designs: Jenny Jensen Greenleaf
Photography: Peter Cunningham
Illustrations: Kimberly Fox and Marjorie Martinelli
Composition: Publishers' Design and Production Services, Inc.
Manufacturing: Steve Bernier

Printed in the United States of America on acid-free paper
22 21 20 19   RWP   2 3 4 5

Acknowledgments

WE'VE WRITTEN THIS UNIT in appreciation of kindergarten teachers near and far—who welcome the littlest of children into their classroom and recognize their unending possibilities as readers and writers, and most importantly, people. You invite children into the world of school, the world of writing, and the world of reading. You help them know that their stories, their words, and their ideas matter. You do this while also managing runny noses, untied shoes, and spilled juice. Your job is difficult, it is big, and above all, it is important.

We want to thank our leader, Lucy Calkins, who nudged us to rethink our best ideas, question existing traditions, and create our best writing work—even when this wasn't easy. You continue to push us, always, to have high expectations of ourselves and for children. You both assisted in the writing of this book and coached us to be better writers. We are grateful for your mentorship.

Thanks also to Katie Clements who joined Lucy in helping us to write this with clarity and power. Your suggestions and your willingness to share the pen helped bring this book to life.

Without the ideas and inspiration of Natalie Louis, Amanda Hartman, Shanna Schwartz, and Rebecca Cronin, this unit wouldn't be what it is. Thank you for the joy, creativity, and happiness you bring to this work. Thank you for brainstorming with us, and for bringing your best ideas to us.

Kim Fox, your artwork never ceases to make us smile. But even more importantly, it provides students with access to and reminders of the important strategies they are learning as writers. Thank you for sharing your talents and your friendship. Peter Cunningham's magical pictures make a big difference, too.

To our daily thought partners—primary staff developers at The Reading and Writing Project: we are infinitely grateful to you. In emails, texts, and around tables, your ideas, practices, and encouragement make this work worth doing. And you make it fun.

Thanks to the primary staff developers at TCRWP for a decade of work thinking through this unit. For many years, this unit was called *Looking Closely*, and it was a unit that invited youngsters to study autumn leaves. We altered the focus in this book, but much of our teaching borrows on the work the organization has done for decades. Then, too, our work on small groups stands on the shoulders of the late Kathleen Tolan, our work with spelling stands on the shoulders of the Units of Study in Phonics, and our work with curriculum in general is steeped in the methods and traditions of our organization. We're especially grateful to the senior leaders at the Project on whose shoulders we stand: Amanda Hartman, Laurie Pessah, Mary Ehrenworth, Colleen Cruz, and of course, Lucy. You inspire us to bring this work near and far to teachers and students. You help us outgrow ourselves.

A special thank you to schools and teachers across the country who piloted early and later iterations of this unit. Namely, the rock-star kindergarten team at Armstrong Elementary in Dallas, TX, our colleague Sara Veltri in Michigan, Yana Karasik at PS 139, Grace Lampon and Teresa Policastro at PS 48, and Kathleen Fanning at PS 682 in Brooklyn. A special thank you to the teachers and staff at PS 9 and PS 15, where many of the photos in this book were taken.

The team at Heinemann has brought equal verve and talent to this effort, and the book is far better because of their help. We thank, especially, our editor Karen Kawaguchi for her impeccable attention to detail and clarity and for being our cheerleader. Elizabeth Valway is a miracle worker behind the scenes, and her prowess with production makes all the difference. Thank you to Shannon Thorner for helping us put it all together. Abby Heim, who directs all things related to this work at Heinemann, has been endlessly patient and helpful to us. We are thrilled to be passing the project of this book on to Lisa Bingen who will bring her sparkle to the effort, helping the whole world to know of the book's arrival. Thank you, thank you.

Friends and family have lent us the time, space, and encouragement needed to take on a project as big as this. Max Rosenberg, thank you for being the supportive partner you are, day in and day out. To the writing group, Eric Hand, Katy Wishow, Ed Hodson, Emily Alverson, and Mike Ochs, thank you for your feedback, laughter, and encouragement.

And to every kindergartener who shows off a glittery band aid on a paper cut, a new backpack, a favorite stuffy, or joyfully-made picture. Thank you for being you.

—Marie and Lizzie

Contents

Acknowledgments • iii

Welcome to the Unit • vii

BEND I Writing Is a Way to Show and Tell

1. Drawing and Writing a Lot on Each Page • 2

Today you'll teach students that as they grow as writers, the amount they draw and write on each page needs to keep growing, too. You will demonstrate how to draw and write a lot on each page: plan a drawing, sketch it quickly, add details, and then write several labels.

2. Writers Plan What They'll Draw and Write • 7

Today you'll teach students that when writers want to draw something on the page, they first think about how they'll draw it and what parts they see. Then they draw the parts and label them. You'll demonstrate how you think before drawing, emphasizing that it helps to draw the object big enough so that you can add details.

3. Returning to a Page to Add More • 12

Today you'll teach students that writers return to their writing to put more on the page. You'll invite kids to think along as you look back at your own writing, thinking aloud and noticing ways to add more pictures and words by telling where something is and what's going on.

4. Writers Use Everything They Know to Spell Words and Don't Wait to Be Perfect • 18

Today you'll teach students that writers try their best to write words on the page, even if they know the words are not spelled exactly right. You will demonstrate how to spell words by using all the tools in the room—the name wall, the alphabet chart, and the snap word chart.

5. Writing Partners Can Help Us Celebrate and Add More • 24

Today you'll teach students that writing partners can help each other find ways to make their writing better. You will demonstrate how to work with a writing partner—put one book in the middle, read and talk, ask questions, and add more.

BEND II Writing Show-and-Tell Books

6. Writers Write Show-and-Tell Books about Important Places • 31

Today you'll teach students that writers can tell about topics, like important places and things, by thinking about the parts of the topic and drawing and writing about them on pages in a book.

7. Writers Make Time for Drawing *and* Writing • 37

Today you'll teach students that writers make time for writing words. For a day or two, it may help to set aside time for writing words so that children remember to do this.

8. Writers and Illustrators Make Decisions • 43

Today you'll teach students that writers make decisions about the ways they put their pictures and words on the page. You'll demonstrate by showing students how you study a page, thinking aloud about the way the pictures and the words are laid out—and how you might try these ways with the class book.

9. Adding Longer Labels to Bring Pages to Life • 50

Today you'll teach students that writers put more details on their pages by adding more words. You'll work with children to study a page of a demonstration text to find places to bring the page to life with longer labels. Then you'll ask children to generate longer labels for their own writing.

10. Writing Sentences that Say What Pictures and Labels Can't • 56

Today you'll teach students that writers can touch their page and say a sentence that tells what the whole page is about. Then they try their best to write that sentence, one word at a time. You'll demonstrate how you think about a sentence and then write that sentence, using all you know about spelling.

11. Growing Writers Talk about Their Writing in Important Ways • 61

Today you'll teach students that writers talk about their writing by sharing what they are making, what they are proud of, and what is tricky. You'll demonstrate how writers do this, role-playing both teacher and writer.

BEND III   Using Patterns to Write Show-and-Tell Books

12. Writing Books that Kids Want to Read • 68

Today you'll teach writers that they can write books that they wish existed in the world—about the people, places, and things that matter to them. You'll channel the class to write a class book together about a topic that's important to kids.

13. Talking and Writing with Patterns and Snap Words • 73

Today you'll teach writers they can write pattern books using high-frequency words. You'll demonstrate by using the high-frequency word chart to think about how a book could go.

14. Studying How Sentences Look • 80

Today you'll guide students to study the conventions of a sentence. You will help students notice that sentences start with an uppercase letter, contain mostly lowercase letters, have words separated by spaces, and end with a punctuation mark.

15. Slowing Down to Leave Spaces between Words • 86

Today you'll teach writers that they can make their writing easy to read by slowing down to leave spaces between words. You'll demonstrate how you use your finger as a tool to help you leave spaces between words.

16. Writers Write More Sentences on a Page • 91

Today you'll teach writers that they can write more than one sentence on a page by rereading and thinking about what else they can say. You'll demonstrate rereading the class book and using the snap word chart to help you add another sentence.

17. Writers Think about How Their Books Will End • 97

Today you'll teach writers that they can think about the endings of their books. You'll show a mentor text that ends with a big idea and then demonstrate how you draft an ending for the class book.

18. Fancying Up Your Writing • 102

Today you'll teach writers that they can prepare their writing for an audience by making sure their sentences look like a book, adding more sentences, and ensuring that each book has an ending. You'll work with the class to check for these things in the class book before sending children off to try it with their own books.

19. Bookstore Celebration • 107

Today you could teach children that writers can celebrate their writing by sharing their books with other people, showing off books they wrote that are important to them and should exist in the world.

Registration instructions to access the digital resources that accompany this book may be found on p. xii.

Welcome to the Unit

THIS UNIT WILL TEACH YOUR CHILDREN to make texts that are a written version of show-and-tell time, that most iconic kindergarten tradition. Children will bring their hair band or robot or Pokémon card to school and they'll share their objects with each other by drawing and labeling. As the unit evolves, they'll show and tell things that are too big to bring to school—their grandma's apartment, the mall—and they'll teach each other about these cherished things not only through labels, but also through pattern books.

Meanwhile, for you, this is not a unit on the genre of show-and-tell writing—there is no such thing. Instead, this is a unit in which you turn all your children into inventive spellers. Typically, at the start of this unit, you will have some children who use writing time as an opportunity to draw and story-tell. By the end of this unit, your children will hopefully all be writing at least a sentence on each page, and writing many pages a day. The spellings in those pages will vary tremendously. Some children will record most of the salient sounds in the words they "stretch out" and will also spell a dozen high-frequency words correctly, while other children will rely mostly on just a very few consonant sounds in each word. The *process* that children go through to write will vary less. They'll draw, then they'll settle on a word to write, and then they'll cycle through a process that involves saying that word, writing the first part of it, rereading that part and saying also the part of the word that they have yet to write, recording that next bit, and rereading again.

Some of you have taught an earlier iteration of this unit, "Looking Closely: Observing, Labeling, and Listing Like Scientists," from the *If . . . Then . . . Curriculum: Assessment-Based Instruction* book from the Grade K Units of Study in Opinion, Information, and Narrative Writing. It revolved around kids collecting and writing about leaves and other natural items. Originally, we intended for this book to be a full-fledged version of that unit, but as we began holding think tanks with our colleagues to reimagine this unit, we realized that the motivation for kids to write wasn't all that great when they were taking leaves from a pile and writing, "This is a red leaf." Also, the technical vocabulary surrounding nature was getting in the way of kids' attempts at inventive spelling. To say much about a leaf, children needed to learn words such as *stem* and *vein*—and though we love to enrich children's vocabulary, it also feels important that children's first forays into writing value their own language and interests.

This new focus, *show-and-tell* writing, reflects the Teachers College Reading and Writing Project's (TCRWP) awareness that in fabulous kindergarten classrooms across the world, children's lives are welcome. Kindergartens are places where glittery Band-Aids are celebrated. Kids everywhere care very much that their robot has a laser and their pink stuffed dog has puppies that can get unzipped from its stomach. Through discussions with colleagues and experiments in classrooms, we emerged with a brand-new storyline: *show and tell*.

Although the motivation to show and tell a favorite object will be high, some children might still be reluctant to write. They'll say, "I don't know how to write. I don't know how to spell words." Kindergartners the world over have said something similar to their teacher. Know first that this is a sign of growth. Prior to coming to school, those children may well have written on misty mirrors and wet beaches, writing jig-jaggy approximations of adult writing. It's a step ahead for the child to realize that writing is made of actual letters, and that it represents sounds.

Although a child's reluctance to write is understandable and even suggests the child has some awareness of all that goes into writing, your front-and-center goal in this unit will be persuading each child that of course, he or she can write. Yours will be the hand held out that brings each of your students into the literacy club. You'll do that by making your classroom into a place that celebrates effort and approximation rather than perfection and product. You'll teach a growth mind-set as clearly as you'll teach the alphabet.

To do this, the first step is you need to *believe*. You need to teach with a rock-solid firm conviction that yes, all your kids can be writing as best they can. In schools across the globe, in communities that include the most high-need urban and rural schools imaginable, we have seen entire classes of kindergarten children become writers by the end of this unit. Their writing will usually be hard to read and may include squiggles in place of some letters, but children can isolate the word they want to write, say it slowly, segmenting and isolating at least some of its constituent sounds. They can record those sounds as best they can onto the page. This work provides youngsters with absolutely vital opportunities to work on phonemic awareness—on segmenting and blending and manipulating sounds. As children work to record sounds, they practice and learn letter-sound correspondence. The writing workshop can also be called the phonics workshop.

The writing workshop could also be called the reading workshop. As children write, they learn the concepts of print. They learn left-to-right, top-to-bottom tracking. They develop a concept of letter and word and of one-to-one. They learn to point under a word and to read that word—first, letter by letter with cumulative blending, then part by part. For now, your children's writing will march ahead of their reading and open the pathway for reading to develop.

Drawing and storytelling will also be important parts of your workshop, and your children can learn skills and habits that are crucial to their growth as they draw and as they talk. They'll learn that writers see their subject in their mind's eye with great precision. Then they put a reproduction of that image onto their page, striving to capture their subject with enough accuracy and detail that someone else, reading what they've put on the page, can conjure up the intended subject. They'll learn it helps to plan this work: Where on the page should this go? How big should it be? What color will work best? They'll learn, too, that revision helps, and that writers shift from pulling in to make something, to pulling back to assess, and then returning, this time to revise.

The challenge as you teach this unit will not be for you to grasp the content of the unit—it will be for you to bring each child along. If some children are reluctant to write, it will be important to hold a mirror up to your teaching and to ask yourself, "Might I inadvertently be sending the message that kids can't write?" Are there people in the room who spell words for students, suggesting that youngsters can't rely on their own work to spell as best they can? Perhaps an aide, a "helpful" parent, or your more confident students are doing that. Anytime someone other than the writer spells or writes on that writer's page, the message is sent that the writer requires another person to encode words. That tells students that they are not part of the literacy club yet.

You might also examine how you're teaching students to stretch words out. Are you stretching the word out for the writer rather than getting her to say the word slowly, stretching it out? If you are doing the work for the child, you are teaching dependence. Beyond that, you're depriving the child of a crucial opportunity to develop phonemic awareness. Teach your writers to stretch out words. If they need help, show them that they can say a word, slowly touching down their arm, saying each part of the word. Or help them pretend there's a rubber band between their hands that they are pulling slowly.

It will be equally important to make sure your classroom is a place where students embrace mistakes with open arms. Compliment effort, giving shout-outs for students who could otherwise be your most reluctant. "Guess what, everyone! Sammy used to say that he couldn't write, but look what he just did! He worked hard, used the alphabet chart, and wrote a word right here! Hurrah, Sammy!"

How important it is that you change Sammy's inner dialogue from "I can't write, I'm not a writer" to "If I work at this, I can do it"! The stories that you tell a child about the work you and that child do together will matter. After helping a child write a word, you can name the procedure in a way that eliminates your role. Say something like, "Wow, did you see how you did that? You said the word slowly, again and again, looked at the alphabet and then wrote the letters you heard! I bet you can do that every time you want to write a hard word!"

When students are first recording letters for the sounds they hear, you'll want to encourage all their attempts. They might look to you to see if they are right or not, and they might come right out and ask, "Is that right?" You'll want to turn the question back to them, saying something like, "What do you think? Say it again. Did you get all the sounds?" If they say yes, encourage them to write more words. This response completes the message that they are the boss of their writing.

You need not worry that your kids will memorize incorrect spellings. Think about it this way. When a child is learning to read and she sees a word and says it incorrectly, you aren't tempted to ask her to stop trying to read, lest she fixate on those errors. Instead, you know that approximations are part and parcel of learning. The necessity of approximation in writing is no different—although the existence of a product that looks "wrong" can make it harder for you to embrace the natural normal learning process in writing than in reading. It is important that you learn to look at a child's invented spellings as they evolve over time and to see progress, rather than errors.

OVERVIEW OF THE UNIT

Kindergarten teachers know that in addition to focused minilessons and time to write independently, five-year-olds need lots of guided practice—the time when we write *with* kids is critical. This unit has interactive writing sessions in the shares and small groups. You'll want to ensure that you write with kids during other parts of the days and weeks, as well. You can label the math center, or write a letter home to parents inviting them to an open house, or make class books in social studies about what families eat. Sharing the pen as you write high-frequency words and listen for letter sounds will give kids more power when they work on their own writing. In thousands of TCRWP classrooms, teachers take the books they've made with their class and make copies of them to put in students' book bins for kids to practice reading during reading workshop.

Bend I: Writing Is a Way to Show and Tell

During the first bend, you'll invite kids to do something they know well—to show and tell about the things that are important to them. On Day One, they'll choose anything nearby—their sock or their backpack—and draw and label it on the page. For the next day, you'll invite children to bring in a special object and this object—a favorite dinosaur, head band, or game—will be the center of their show-and-tell writing for the remainder of the bend. The big work of the bend involves drawing that object part by part, writing lots of labels onto that drawing, and then revising the picture and the labels by adding more onto them.

By the end of the first bend, your goal will be for kids to be writing more than ever. You'll rally kids to achieve this goal by showing a "time capsule" of their work from earlier in the year, asking how their writing has improved. You'll rally your students to be brave spellers and co-create a "Brave Spellers" anchor chart with them through interactive writing. You'll celebrate moments when a child attempts to write a word, even if the resulting spelling doesn't look like the ones in a book. You'll remind your children to use helpful tools such as the name wall, the alphabet chart, and their collection of snap words. (We use the term *snap words* when we talk about or teach high-frequency words to children.)

This bend aligns perfectly to Bend I of *Word Scientists: Using the Alphabet Chart to Start*, the second kindergarten unit in the Units of Study in Phonics—but this book can also be taught in a self-contained way.

Bend II: Writing Show-and-Tell Books

The second bend channels students to write lots of books about places they love. You'll tell children that although these places are impossible to bring to show and tell at school, when they write about these places, they can still share them. To write a book about the mall or the park or Grandma's house, the writer first has to decide what part of those topics goes on page 1, what part on page 2, what part on page 3. Throughout their school careers, whenever your children tackle expository writing, they'll draw on skills that they learn during this portion of the unit as they divide their beloved places into chunks that can be captured across the pages of a book. Perhaps the book about the mall highlights a few favorite stores, one on each page. Then again, it might contain just the best parts of the mall: the escalator, the merry-go-round in the food court, and the bathrooms with foamy soap. The book about the park might have one page for the lake with ducks, one page for the playing fields, one for the walking paths.

Meanwhile, of course, your children will continue to practice their inventive spelling as they label all that they are attempting to share.

You will teach students that they must make time for writing words and you'll ensure that happens. You'll also engage students in studying a mentor text to see how the author and illustrator put the words and the pictures on the page. This will help them make decisions about their own page layouts. You will channel kids to write longer labels with phrases, and you'll nudge kids who are ready to take on writing sentences. At the end of this bend, you'll teach your kindergartners ways to talk about their writing, as you invite fifth-graders to be a part of the writing time and celebration that day.

Bend III: Using Patterns to Write Show-and-Tell Books

In the final bend, your goal will be to get kids writing lots of sentences across pages, while learning and using high-frequency words. You'll set the stage by inviting kids to turn the classroom into a book factory—a place to write the books that represent topics that are important to real kids. The momentum of this bend will be driven by the countdown to the last day of the unit, when you'll turn your classroom into a bookstore where kids share their books with a wider audience.

Children will learn that when they write books for kids, it can help to write in a pattern using the words they know in a snap—high-frequency words. They'll think of a topic, say their sentences across pages, and then draw and write their book. Know that once kids can write one sentence on a page, they are ready to write more than one sentence, and you'll teach them to do so.

Toward the end of this bend, your children will fancy up a few books and make them "bookstore ready." You'll turn the classroom charts into a sort of checklist, starring the particular parts of charts that writers should pay special attention to as they return to their books and publish them. To culminate the unit, students will celebrate by transforming the room into a bookstore. They'll make sections in the classroom for the books they've written, signs inviting people to the store, a cash register for people to buy the books, and a read-aloud area for kids to read their books aloud to their classmates and the adults you invite to participate.

ASSESSMENT

This additional writing unit is designed to follow *Launching the Writing Workshop*, the first kindergarten unit of the Units of Study in Opinion, Information, and Narrative Writing. Ideally, you will have collected student work from the first few days of school to use as a baseline to show the enormous growth we expect students to make during this unit. If you weren't able to do that, you now may want to collect a writing sample from your students, selecting a text that doesn't reflect teacher involvement. We call this on-demand writing. While we generally recommend using a formal writing prompt from *Writing Pathways*, for this unit, you might find it more helpful to conduct an informal on-demand. You might say, "Take the next few minutes to write about something that's important to you. Remember to draw the picture and write the words."

To later ascertain if there is a logic to children's invented spellings, it will be helpful if you have a record of what it was that each child intended to say. If you know that a child who has written *ILTUM* intended to write *I love the mall*, then you can study the line of letters and see evidence of some early

knowledge. Just ask pleasantly, "What are you writing?" and jot down whatever the child says, keeping that correctly spelled version away from the child's eyes. You can probably scrawl the dictation in cursive onto a Post-it® and stick it on the backside of the child's writing. If the child notices at all, you might say, "Oh, that's just some notes to myself." Don't worry about getting this sort of a transcript for every child, nor about your records being complete. Any information you can get will be helpful, but it won't be possible to do this with perfection. You will want to keep these on-demand samples, perhaps in a time capsule or on a bulletin board, to return to again and again so that students can see their growth.

Another way to inform your teaching will be to collect students' writing folders at the end of *Launching the Writing Workshop*. Consider the volume of student writing (how many pieces and how many words they've written) and their attempts at representational drawings, labels, and sentences.

Your students' foundational skills will be paramount as you enter and move through the unit. If your students' writing does not tell you what they know about spelling, you may hand out a sheet of paper with a few pictures on it and ask students to label it—like a brief spelling quiz. This will enable you to get a much-needed sense of where students are in their spelling ability or transcription development. You'll want to refer to "A Progression of Spelling Development" in the online resources for Session 10 to assess students' spelling development stage. Once you identify their stage of development, you can support them in getting to the next level. This unit is designed to help your whole class move along this progression, from writing strings of letters to sentences.

In addition to looking at student work, you will want to have assessed students' alphabet knowledge, high-frequency word knowledge, and concepts of print. Look to the resources on the TCRWP website or in the Units of Study in Phonics for an alphabet assessment, concepts of print assessment, and high-frequency word assessments.

You will be assessing not only this unit, but also your phonics instruction. We strongly believe that every school needs to teach a research-based, sequenced phonics curriculum, and that curriculum needs to support transfer into reading and writing. If many of your kids are not writing sentences by the end of this unit, look to see whether your phonics instruction is keeping apace of your writing and reading instruction. Remember that presumably your students will be reading level C books containing a wide range of high-frequency words and even beginning digraphs by the spring. You won't want your phonics curriculum to lag behind your reading and your writing curriculum, as phonics is only important insofar as it supports transfer to writing and reading.

GETTING READY

Since this is the second unit of the year, we expect that prior to the start of this unit, you already have a writing workshop up and running in your classroom, with a place in the room where children can go to choose the paper on which they'll write. In the first bend, you'll offer the option of single sheets of blank paper, plus paper that contains a large box and some lines. In Bends II and III, you'll channel children to write on stapled booklets, each of which contains a cover page and several pages. Each page contains a box for drawing and some lines for writing. You'll want to offer some choices—perhaps some of those booklets have more lines for writing, or more pages. To launch Bend II, since students will be moving from single pages to booklets, and to avoid a logjam at your writing center, you might put a stack of blank booklets on the center of tables or hand a booklet to each student during the link of the lesson. For subsequent books, put adequate supplies of booklets in the writing center and set up a routine so kids know to go to the writing center to get new booklets. Look to this unit's online resources for paper choice samples.

Prior to this unit, your students may already have writing folders in which they store their work, perhaps with a red dot for the "done" side and a green dot for the "still working" side. Many teachers find it helpful to provide each table with writing caddies containing pens, Post-its, revision strips, scissors, tape, and glue for students to use when they are writing and making revisions on the tables. Pencils are a possible option, but your children will find it easier to write with pens and the writing they produce will be easier for them and you to read. You won't in any case want them to be erasing, as the sequence of work they do will be important evidence of learning.

To support students with moving through the writing process, you'll continue to display the "When We Are Done We Have Just Begun!" anchor chart from *Launching the Writing Workshop*.

Before starting this unit, you will want to send a letter home to parents asking them to send in an object for students to write about. You may set some ground rules for what the object should be—small enough to fit in a gallon plastic, zip top bag, not too costly, and something that students can keep in school for a few days. Also choose your own object to model with—a stuffed animal or childhood toy. In case some students forget to bring something, gather a few stuffed animals, action figures, cars—anything high-interest for students to write about.

To reinforce the phonics work your students are doing in this unit, display your alphabet chart prominently. We recommend that you place a mini alphabet chart in each child's folder as well. As part of helping your students learn their letters, be sure you've created a name wall with students' names and pictures in alphabetical order. If you are using the Units of Study in Phonics, you will have already done this in the first unit.

Be ready to continue to support your students' work with high-frequency words by adding them to a high-frequency word chart or wall. When teaching kids high-frequency words, we often refer to them as *snap words* because we want kids to know them "in a snap." There are two kinds of high-frequency words: 1) words that can be decoded, following a predictable spelling pattern like *me*, *can*, *look*, and 2) words that *cannot* be decoded, do not follow a spelling pattern, and must be memorized, like *come*, *the*, *of*. If you are using the Units of Study in Phonics alongside this unit, your students will be gaining familiarity with words such as *me*, *the*, *a*, *I*, *like*, *my*, *see*, *at*, *look*, *this*, *is*, *here*, *an*, *it*, *in*, *and*. You might add a few more high-frequency words like *can*, *are*, and *to* to your snap word chart during Bend II to support students' pattern book writing.

If you are not using the Units of Study in Phonics, be sure to begin teaching these words as soon as possible. You may want to look at the Session 1 share for suggestions on how to teach high-frequency words. You can find a printable list of these words in the online resources for Session 13. You might provide students with high-frequency word cards to keep in a baggie or envelope in their writing folders or at their desks. (We provide printable high-frequency word cards on the online resources for Session 16.)

Looking ahead in the unit, there are two big events to prepare for. In Session 11, we suggest you celebrate students' growth by inviting fifth-graders into your room to talk to your students about their writing. Of course, these needn't be fifth-graders—children from another grade will do! You will want to schedule about a half an hour for these children to be in your room with your students as they write.

The second event is the celebration at the end of the unit. For this last day, we suggest you transform your classroom into a bookstore and invite parents and school community members. We suggest scheduling this day now, so you have a clear end time for your unit and students have something to work toward. Scheduling this ahead of time allows you to gather materials and to invite an adult or two beforehand to help students get ready.

Know that the celebration we imagine is just one option, and you may very well think of a different way to celebrate. Be sure to share your ideas on the writing Units of Study Facebook page, where 32,000 other teachers will be eager to learn from your ingenuity. Those teachers will be ready to help you, so turn to that community with your questions.

You'll want to collect some mentor texts for students to refer to during this unit. For the first two bends, look to high-interest nonfiction with flaps and exciting illustrations. You'll want to have a couple of options ready to show kids during Session 8. You'll see that we demonstrate with one of our favorites, *The Ultimate Book of Vehicles: From Around the World* by Anne-Sophie Baumann and Didier Balicevic. We also love:

My Fridge: My First Book of Food (Duopress Labs)

On the Go by Roger Priddy

Best Little Word Book Ever by Richard Scarry

My First Farm: Let's Get Working! by Dawn Sirett

The Big Book of Bugs by Yuval Zommer

To prepare for Bend III, gather lots of patterned concept books to read aloud and show kids as inspiration for the pattern books they'll be creating. We suggest you look in your level A and B baskets for books with a predictable pattern and many high-frequency words. For Session 17, you'll need books with a pattern change on the last page. Some of our favorites are:

Best Friends by Tina Athaide

Daisy's Party Dresses by Michele Dufresne

Look at Me! by Eleanor Flegg

Moms by Matthew Hugo

The Zoo by Rose Lewis

The Go-Karts (Rigby PM)

Now by Antoinette Portis

ONLINE DIGITAL RESOURCES

A variety of resources to accompany this unit are available in the online resources, including charts and examples of student work shown throughout *Show and Tell Writing*, as well as links to other electronic resources. Offering daily support for your teaching, these materials will help you provide a structured learning environment that fosters independence and self-direction.

To access and download all the digital resources for this unit:

1. Go to www.heinemann.com and click the link in the upper right to log in. (If you do not have an account yet, you will need to create one.)
2. Enter the following registration code in the box to register your product: WUOS_HSLB0
3. Enter the security information requested.
4. Once you have registered your product it will appear in the list of My Online Resources.

(You may keep copies of these resources on up to six of your own computers or devices. By downloading the file, you acknowledge that they are for your individual or classroom use and that neither the resources not the product code will be distributed or shared.)

Writing Is a Way to Show and Tell

BEND I

Session 1

Drawing and Writing a Lot on Each Page

GETTING READY

✓ You may want to wear interesting socks to class so you can draw and write about them (see Teaching).

✓ You'll need chart paper and markers to demonstrate drawing and writing (see Teaching).

✓ Display the new anchor chart, "To Show and Tell" (see Link).

✓ Be sure your alphabet chart and name wall are accessible to students (see Mid-Workshop Teaching).

✓ Display the "How to Learn a Word" anchor chart from Kindergarten Unit 1, *Making Friends with Letters*, of the Units of Study in Phonics series (see Share).

✓ Remind children to bring a favorite object from home tomorrow to draw and write about. You will also need to bring a favorite object (see Share).

IN THIS SESSION

TODAY YOU'LL teach students that as they grow as writers, the amount they draw and write on each page needs to keep growing, too. You will demonstrate how to draw and write a lot on each page: plan a drawing, sketch it quickly, add details, and then write several labels.

TODAY YOUR STUDENTS will think and talk about what they'll be drawing and writing about. Then they'll choose one thing to write about and they'll draw and write about that one item, filling up one page with a picture and labels. In the share, children will learn the word *my* so they can begin to add it to their labels.

MINILESSON

CONNECTION

Celebrate that your students are growing—and that growth includes growth as writers.

"Writers, will you come to the meeting area and bring your writing folders?" Once children had gathered, I asked them to sit on their folders for now.

"Writers, when Samantha came into the classroom today, I stopped in my tracks. And you know what I said? I said, 'Samantha, you are growing!' Since the beginning of the year, she has gotten taller right before my eyes.

"But you know what? Just now, as you came over to the meeting area, I realized Samantha is not the only one who is growing. You all are! I mean, holy moly! Your arms and legs are getting so long that some of your clothes don't fit. Your parents must be saying 'Slow down. You are growing too fast!'

"Here's the exciting thing. You aren't just growing as people—you are also growing as readers and writers. Do you realize that at the start of our year, most of you didn't know that you write the letter *M* for the /m/ sound? Now your pockets are full of alphabet letters that you know and can use."

Suggest that because the kids have grown so much, it is time for a new unit. Rally them around the idea of a unit devoted to show and tell and get them started on today's show and tell.

"Because you have grown so much, it's time for us to start a whole new unit during writing workshop. I've been thinking maybe this could be a *show-and-tell* unit. That would mean that each of you would need to bring in a special thing—maybe a special stuffed animal, or a cool hair band, or an action figure—and then you'd use writing to show and tell about that thing.

"For today, instead of bringing something from home, we'll need to choose our show-and-tells from what we have right here. You know what's cool? There's a lot to tell even just about the things you are wearing. I have things to tell you about my socks—that might sound funny, but these socks have little dolphins on them, so I like them."

❖ **Name the teaching point.**

"Today I want to teach you that because you are growing as writers, the amount of stuff you put on each page of your writing needs to grow, too. Starting now and for the rest of your life, it's important for you to draw and write *a lot* on each page."

We find that kids write more when they have emotional ties to what they are writing about. For tomorrow's lesson, you'll encourage kids to bring in things that are special to them.

TEACHING

Demonstrate how you write a lot on each page. Start by planning a drawing, sketching super quickly, adding detail.

"So writers, watch me do this new kind of writing. Watch especially to see how I get a *lot* on each page. In a minute, you'll be able to plan the way you are going to get a lot on each of your pages."

I picked up a marker and turned the chart paper to a new page. I looked at my socks, and said, "Hmm, . . . I first need to draw my socks. I have to decide if I'll make me with socks on or just socks." Instead of thinking through the answer, I took twenty seconds to sketch myself, wearing socks. "What else?" I asked. I added details—little dolphins—onto the socks.

Debrief that you added a lot to your drawing. Then proceed to label half a dozen things on your drawing.

"Did you notice that I added details to my drawing? Now watch how I'm going to write, too." I said "me" and wrote that, then said "What else?" I labeled the blue stripe on my sock. To write *blue*, I said the word, isolated the first sound, recorded that sound, then said the word again and captured more sounds. I continued, adding a few more labels to my drawing.

You'll see that we purposely do this quickly. You will be teaching into each of these parts over the course of the bend. This is not the moment to teach the correct spelling of a word like stripe. *You are teaching the process of fearlessly capturing the sounds that one hears in a word. You'll bring home that point best by modeling inventive spelling.*

SESSION 1: DRAWING AND WRITING A LOT ON EACH PAGE

ACTIVE ENGAGEMENT

Channel writers to think and talk about what they'll be drawing and writing about. Help them think of possible ideas by sharing a few things you could have written about but didn't.

"So writers, I know that while I was drawing and labeling my socks, you were thinking about what you have on that you could tell others about. I could have written about my sweater because I love the buttons and my grandma gave it to me, or about these silver and black shoes. Right now, will you and your partner talk about what you could, maybe, draw and write about?"

As children talked, I oohed and ahhed over their ideas. "Oh, you must tell about that!" I said over and over. "Whew! What an idea!"

LINK

Send children off to choose one thing to write about, then to draw and write about that one item, filling up one page.

"Writers, in a few days, I'm going to ask you to look at the writing you have done this week and to compare it with the writing you did earlier this year to see how much your writing has grown. Your goal will be to put a *lot* more details and a *lot* more words onto each page of your writing. For now, you are going to work all day on just one page of writing."

I revealed a new anchor chart, "To Show and Tell." "You can start by looking and thinking of something you are wearing, something that you could tell others about. Then you'll put that thing—that sweater, that shoe, that backpack—onto your page. I can't wait to see all you'll draw and write today! Off you go!"

Think strategically about who your students are talking to on the rug—designating rug spots helps students know who their partner is. If you have students who are in the silent phase of English language acquisition, you can put them in a group of three, so that they have language models.

You'll refer to this chart over the next few days, so be sure to display it prominently in your room.

CONFERRING AND SMALL-GROUP WORK

Rally Children to Write and Draw about Themselves

TEACHERS, YOU'LL PUT YOUR ROLLER SKATES ON TODAY, moving quickly among your students so as to rally them each to draw and write. Early on, the challenge will be to help kids embrace the notion of writing about a sweater or a pair of shoes. Those aren't the most exciting topics on earth, so your appreciative support for them will be a big deal. You might walk around to different tables, offering compliments and encouragement:

- *To a child who has just drawn the outline of the object:* "I was hoping you'd write about that sweater. I love the collar on it. Be sure you add that in!"

- *To a child who is just sitting there:* "I was wondering about those sneakers. Where did you get them? What I notice are the sparkles, right? So cool!" Tap their writing paper and move on.

- *When a child doesn't want to write about what they are wearing:* "I was wondering about your knapsack. This thing hanging off the zipper is so cool."

Now is not the time to channel kids to choose topics they really care about. These are one-day topics only. If you need to do so, you could quietly allow a few kids to think about toys they're apt to bring from home and to get started on those a day before the rest of the class.

Conferring to Build a Growth Mind-set

If some kids act as if the challenge today is hard, welcome that and help kids develop the growth mind-set needed to tackle the challenge. You might pull up next to a writer who has stopped writing and drawing and say, "It *is* a challenge, isn't it! But I know you. You love a good challenge, don't you? It's no different than when you ride that scooter of yours. When you reach a hill, do you just say, 'I give up. This is hard'? No way! You keep working. You keep trying!" By reminding them of how they've overcome obstacles in other parts of their lives, you are creating a growth-mind-set narrative for students. Your goal is to get students to see themselves as hard workers, not perfect drawers or spellers. You want them to see that by making mistakes they are growing. Be sure you are praising effort, not accuracy.

Take opportunities to learn more about your students to support their growth mind-set. You could go around to each student and ask them "What do you love to do outside of school?" Then, follow it up with "What do you do when that thing gets hard?" Jot their answers down for yourself so later on you can make connections for students between how they've solved problems outside of school and how they can solve any issues they face in school.

MID-WORKSHOP TEACHING   **Celebrate Tools that Help—the Name Wall and the Alphabet Chart**

"Eyes on me, writers! Let me tell you what Amara did. She said, 'I don't know how to spell *hair band*.' Then Joshua said, 'You should use the alphabet chart!' Then guess what? Amara tried! She said the word slowly until she heard the first sound. She didn't give up! Look at how many words she got down on her paper." I held up Amara's paper. "Like if you want to write *toe*, you need to say that word slowly over and over until you hear the first sound: /t/, /t/, /t/—*toe!*. Then you can write *T*.

"Right now, will you stop drawing—and every one of you, will you work on your writing? Work on writing labels. Remember, you can check the name wall and the alphabet chart to figure out how to get a word onto the paper. I'll be coming around to admire your work."

SESSION 1: DRAWING AND WRITING A LOT ON EACH PAGE

SHARE

Writing More Words on Your Papers—*My*

Channel children to learn the word *my* so they can add it to their drawings.

"Writers, wow, that was fun! Put your writing in the 'still working' or 'done' side of your folder and join me in the meeting area. I saw some of you label your picture with the word *me*. If you are in your picture, you can do that. Sometimes your picture doesn't show *you*, it only shows your sweater or your shirt. So let me teach you one more word that you will want to use: *my*," I said, and labeled my drawing "My Socks." I underlined the word *my* in the label.

"Will you do all the things you know to do to learn *my* so that you can use it anytime, in a snap? I brought out the "How to Learn a Word" anchor chart.

"First, let's read the word *my*." I pointed under it and read the word with the class. "Now let's study it. Turn and tell your partner what you notice about it. How many letters does it have? What does it start and end with?"

I shared what I heard. "Yes, it has two letters, and it starts the same as *me*. It has a small letter and a longer letter that goes below the line. It ends with the letter *Y*, but it sounds like *I*. Let's spell the word and write the letters in the air as we do it." We said the letters and wrote the words in the air with our fingers.

"Let's use the word *my* in a sentence. Are you ready? Turn and tell your partner as many sentences as you can think of with the word *my*." I heard sentences like these: "This is my sneaker." "I love my sweater." "Here is my special marker." I brought students back together and said, "I'm going to add *my* to our snap word collection. That way you can use it your writing."

Invite writers to bring in a show-and-tell object for tomorrow's lesson.

"Writers, I want to remind you that tomorrow, you are going to want to bring in something you care about to show and tell in your writing. Make it something small—we don't have lots of shelf space—and something *you* know is special, even if other people may not think so. It could be a card you got from your grandma, or your favorite toy car, or a stuffed animal with only one eye because you've had it for such a long time. Will you tell someone near you what you might bring in? Turn and talk."

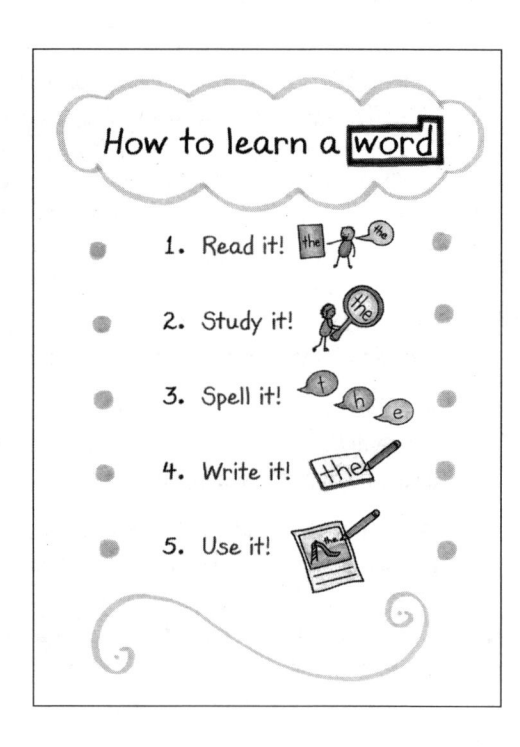

How to learn a word

1. Read it!
2. Study it!
3. Spell it!
4. Write it!
5. Use it!

Session 2

Writers Plan What They'll Draw and Write

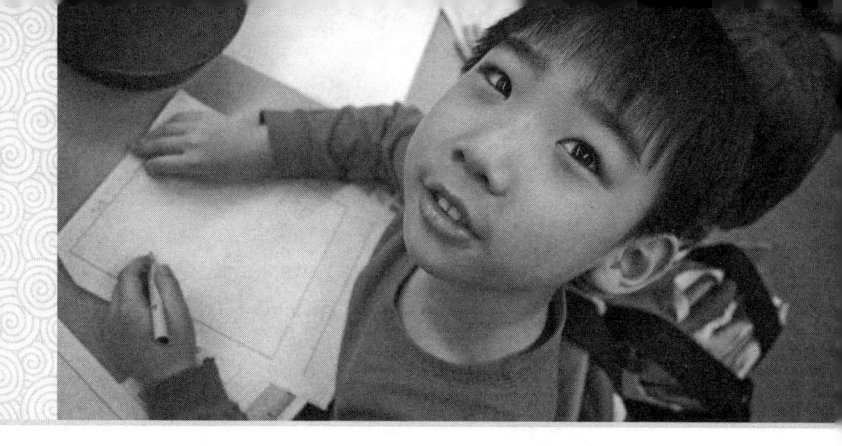

IN THIS SESSION

TODAY YOU'LL teach students that when writers want to draw something on the page, they first think about how they'll draw it and what parts they see. Then they draw the parts and label them. You'll demonstrate how you think before drawing, emphasizing that it helps to draw the object big enough so that you can add details.

TODAY YOUR STUDENTS will draw their objects, thinking about the parts they see. Then, they'll label their drawings, saying words slowly, listening for sounds, and recording letters for the sounds they hear.

GETTING READY

- Be sure that you and your children have brought a "special object" from home to draw and write about today. The example in this session is a stuffed bunny, but you can bring any object with kid-appeal (see Connection, Teaching, and Active Engagement).

- Prepare chart paper and markers to demonstrate drawing and writing (see Teaching and Active Engagement).

- Refer to the anchor chart that you introduced the day before, "To Show and Tell" (see Link).

MINILESSON

CONNECTION

Recruit students to set up their writing spots, getting their special objects and placing them at their spots ready for them to use after the lesson.

"Did some of you remember to bring something to school that you want to show and tell? If you didn't, no matter—you can still draw and write about that thing today, and you can bring it tomorrow.

"Right now, before you come to the meeting area, will you get your object out and put it at your writing spot? When your writing spot is all set, come over to the meeting area. You don't need to bring anything but come super quickly because we have exciting work to do."

Once the children had gathered, I said, "I have some tips to teach you about how you can draw and write about what you brought. Will you watch me do that?"

"Here's what I brought," I said, and pulled a small, raggedy, stuffed rabbit from a bag. "It may not look all that special to you, but Bunny is super special to me."

❖ **Name the teaching point.**

"Today I want to teach you that when you want to draw something, it helps to first think, 'How will I draw this? What parts do I see?,' and then to draw all those parts. After that, you can label all the parts."

TEACHING

Demonstrate how you think before drawing, emphasizing that it helps to draw the object big enough so that you can add details.

"Kindergartners, I *could* just pull this rabbit out of my bag and start drawing it," and I began making a teeny-weeny little rabbit in the center of my page, "but if I drew my bunny like this, I couldn't show her eyes or her ribbon or anything because she's too small.

"What I often do is, I look at the parts and think 'What are the parts to this thing?' Then I draw one of them." I looked at the bunny. "I'll start with the head. I'm going to make it big enough that I can add stuff like her mouth." I drew the outline of a rabbit head. Then I looked back at the rabbit and said to the kids, "What's another part that we should draw?" They chimed in with many parts. I took the idea of drawing a body and added that to the head.

ACTIVE ENGAGEMENT

Channel students to think and talk about the other parts of the object they can add to the drawing.

"We can't stop there. What parts do you think we should add next? Turn and tell your partner." Kids whispered to each other that the rabbit needed ears, arms, legs. "Can you make a pretend rabbit on the imaginary paper in front of you and show each other how you'd add those parts into the drawing?" I asked. "I'll listen in and try to do all the things."

I shifted between super-brief stints of eavesdropping and moments of adding the rest of the rabbit's body parts to my drawing.

Recruit students to help you label your drawing, saying words slowly, listening for sounds you hear, and then recording those sounds.

Before completing the rabbit, I called for the group's attention. "Now comes the fun part, right? We get to write words!"

You can model with anything. However, if the item is actually important to you it will be more meaningful to kids. Kids appreciate authenticity in the same way adults do. You might bring in a stuffed animal from childhood, a favorite blanket, or a toy you grew up with.

Leaving space for your students to chime in as you are teaching allows for a higher level of engagement. If students don't call out, continue with the lesson, thinking aloud as you do. It might sound like, "Oh, I could add the body."

FIG. 2–1 Teacher drawing with inventive spelling.

SHOW AND TELL WRITING: FROM LABELS TO PATTERN BOOKS

I continued, "Join me in labeling the bunny. What can we write here?" and I pointed to her ear. We said *ear* slowly, listening for the first sound /ē/ and for any other sounds that we heard. When the children heard the /r/ sound for the letter *R*, I asked one of them to add that to the label.

LINK

Remind students of the work that they will be doing with their objects and refer to the anchor chart.

"I know, I know. You all are dying to get started doing this with your own treasures. Let's remember the work you'll be doing. First, you'll look at your treasure. Then before you draw, you plan. You think, 'How will this go?' You notice the parts and draw them on your page. Then you label." I pointed to the anchor chart from the day before.

If the kids are participating in labeling and the spelling is approximate, that is as expected. Later on, you might rewrite these labels, substituting correct spelling. For now, you are coaching students to hear sounds, so you are inviting invented spellings.

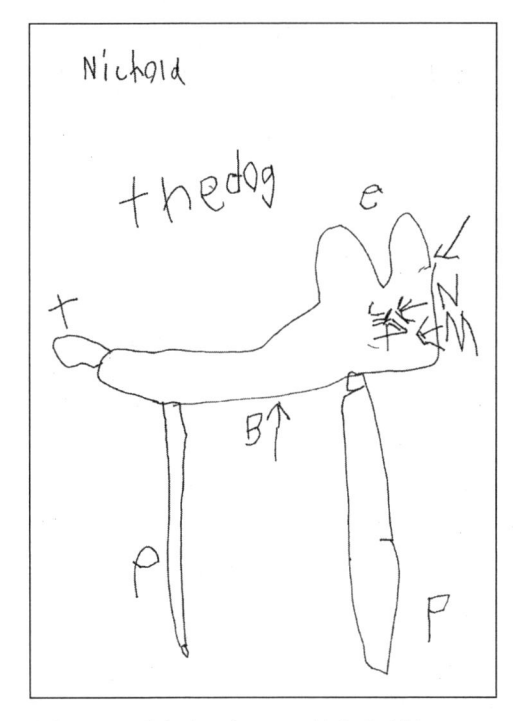

FIG. 2–2   Nicholas drew and labeled his stuffed dog. *(Left to right, top to bottom*: the dog, tail, ears, nose, mouth, body, paw, paw)

FIG. 2–3   Valery drew and wrote about her stuffed chick. *(Left to right, top to bottom*: eyes, mouth, wing, feet, hand, ear)

SESSION 2: WRITERS PLAN WHAT THEY'LL DRAW AND WRITE

CONFERRING AND SMALL-GROUP WORK

Channel High Energy into High Productivity

YOUR MAIN GOAL is to encourage kids to write up a storm, getting as many words down on their page as possible. Shout out attempts that children make as they write words. Praise effort instead of accuracy.

Because everyone will have their toys and other objects out on their tables, they may be more distracted during writing than usual. You might consider providing children with a few minutes of exploration time before writing. During writing, to help them stay focused, you will probably not pull small groups or do conferences with individuals. Instead, you may decide to circle the room, whispering in quick compliments and directions, making sure to keep your own volume low and their productivity high:

- *To students who are playing with their toys.* "I see you looking closely at your object to see all the parts. Let me see you start drawing those parts on your page! Pick up that pen . . . I can't wait to see your drawing!" Gently tap the paper and wait until they pick up their pen, then move away. Check back in on them in a few moments to be sure they got started.
- *To a writer who seems to be staring into space.* "I can see you're ready to draw your picture. Look at your object and get started drawing!"
- *To writers who are talking about their toys.* "I know you're excited to talk about your toys with each other. You'll have time at the end of our workshop to do just that. Now is the time for drawing your picture and writing words so you can teach people who are not in our classroom about our special things." Gently move their papers closer to them and motion for them to get started drawing and writing.
- *To writers who say they are done but have no words on their page.* "When you're done you've just begun! You drew your picture. Did you add your words? Point to your picture, what can you label? Say the word slowly, write down the letters you hear! Use the alphabet chart if you need help."

Holding Table Conferences to Support Getting Words Down on the Page

You can also move from table to table offering more practice to students. You might pause the entire table after chatting with one child and say, "Writers, José was thinking that he'd like to write the word *brave* on his page, to tell about his action figure. Let's try saying the word *brave* slowly together!" As you say the word, slide your hand down your arm slowly. You can then prompt kids to collectively say the word slowly a few times and remind them to do this with more words on their own. Keep in mind your ultimate goal is that kids are saying it slowly *on their own*. It's easy to fall into the trap of stretching for kids, rather than getting them to do it themselves.

MID-WORKSHOP TEACHING **Writing More Words**

"Writers, if you haven't started writing words yet, now is a good time to start. Stop your drawing for now and pick up your pen. When I want to add more words to my writing, it helps to think, 'What is this?' and start by writing the answer.

"Ready to try this? Point to something in your writing and think, 'What is this?' Then write that word. Remember to say the word slowly, over and over, so you can hear the sounds. Then, write the sounds you hear." I coached students to try this a few times, pointing to other things in their drawing and then labeling it.

"Wow, writers! Your readers are going to learn so much about your special treasures because you're adding a lot of words.

"When you're finished with one page about your object, you can choose a different thing to draw and write about. It could be something you're wearing or something in your backpack."

SHOW AND TELL WRITING: FROM LABELS TO PATTERN BOOKS

SHARE

Talk Time
Show and Tell

Rally children to share their stories about their treasures.

"Writers, writing time is over for today. Take a look at your work and decide whether you will put it in the 'done' side or the 'still working' side of your writing folder. Then close your folder and place your object on top, to show that you are ready for our share today." When kids were cleaned up and sitting at their tables, I continued.

"You worked so hard to teach about your special object today—you drew pictures *and* wrote words. You're going to be writing about these special objects for a few more days, and I can tell you have a lot to say about them! And guess what? The more you talk about something, the better you get at writing about it! Right now, will you turn to your partner and tell them everything you can about your object? Tell them where you got it, why you love it so much, and what's special about it."

Once everyone had shared stories about their special objects, I said, "Writers, this work doesn't stop here. You can do this at home, too. I bet your families could tell you stories about your special objects, and then you could add those stories into your writing. Tonight your job is to ask for some stories about your special objects."

Session 3

Returning to a Page to Add More

IN THIS SESSION

TODAY YOU'LL teach students that writers return to their writing to put more on the page. You'll invite kids to think along as you look back at your own writing, thinking aloud and noticing ways to add more pictures and words by telling where something is and what's going on.

TODAY YOUR STUDENTS will begin by returning to the previous day's work to add details to their drawings and words, like where something is or what's going on. After students finish adding on to one page, expect them to start a new page about the same object or another object that includes where something is or what's going on.

GETTING READY

- Think of an author your children know well to help you talk about what great writers do. We refer to Joy Cowley (see Connection).
- Display the "When We Are Done, We Have Just Begun!" anchor chart from Unit 1, *Launching the Writing Workshop*, in the Units of Study in Opinion, Information, and Narrative Writing in the meeting area (see Teaching).
- Be ready to add to the class writing piece you started the day before (see Teaching).
- Display and add to the anchor chart, "To Show and Tell" (see Teaching).
- Students will need their writing folders or a piece of writing for the minilesson (see Active Engagement).
- Create a "Closed" sign for the writing center (see Link).
- You may want to have Elkonin boxes and counters or tokens on hand to give to children (see Conferring and Small-Group Work).
- Cue up the online video of the *Sesame Street* song "What I Am." A link to the video is available in the online resources (see Share).

MINILESSON

CONNECTION

Explain that writers often have projects they return to—and when they do, they make choices about what to do next.

"Kindergartners, a very famous teacher once told me that when you put toys out for kids to play with, it is really important *not* to put too many toys out, because then, you know what kids do? They play for a few minutes with this truck, then a few minutes with this action figure, then a few minutes with this ball. Like, 'Next! Next! Next!' Sometimes, having just one toy is better. Kids come up with so many cool things to do with just one toy!

"I'm telling you that because you *might* look at the writing you did yesterday and think, 'I'm all done with that.'" I wiped my hands off as if to say, "Done." "You might be thinking, 'Next!'

"But here's the thing. *Great* writers don't just write about something for one day and then say, 'I'm all done. What's next?' Do you think Joy Cowley just wrote one little page about Mrs. Wishy-Washy for one day and then said, 'Next!'?

"No way! Instead, Joy Cowley thought to herself, 'What else could I draw and write with Mrs. Wishy-Washy? Where else could she go? What else could she do?'"

Feel free to substitute Joy Cowley with any author your class knows well.

❖ **Name the teaching point.**

"Today I want to teach you that writers aren't always moving on to the next piece, and the next, and the next. Instead, writers often return to their writing and find ways to show and tell even more. Sometimes, to tell more, they tell *where* something is and what's going on."

TEACHING

Invite kids to think along with you as you open your folder to look back at your writing, noticing ways you could add more.

"If we really want to be the kind of writers who don't always say 'Next, next, next . . . ,' that means we'll need to remember the saying on our writing workshop chart, 'When we are done, we have just begun.' We'll need to go back into the 'done' side of our folders or pieces that we think are finished." I pointed to the piece about my bunny that the class had worked on in the previous day's minilesson.

Think aloud, showing your decision-making process for what you might add. Be sure to talk about what you could add in the pictures *and* the words.

"So writers, let's look back at the work I did yesterday, writing about my bunny. Hmm, . . . I already put something on the paper. I must be done, right?" I pushed the page aside dramatically.

Then, acting as if the kids had chorused a protest (even if they hadn't), I paused. "What? You think I can't just move on? That I should try to add on?"

I put the bunny page in front of me. "The thing is, I already did put in all her parts—her nose and all. I already have the details about my topic, my bunny. But wait, now I'm remembering. One way that writers add on to their picture and their story is they tell more about where it is and what's happening around it. My bunny stays on a shelf in my room."

I drew a shelf under the bunny and me next to her, arms out as if to pick her up. I quickly wrote the words *the shelf* and *me*.

"Now I have a lot more to write and draw."

Debrief, and add the new strategy you demonstrated to the anchor chart.

"Writers, do you see what I did? I went back to my writing—and I thought, 'What else could I add?' I added details around my page that showed where something was and what was going on." I added the Post-it for the new strategy, "Add More!" to the "To Show and Tell" anchor chart.

"When We Are Done, We Have Just Begun!" is a chart from Launching the Writing Workshop *in the Units of Study in Opinion, Information, and Narrative Writing. You'll want to quickly introduce it today, if you haven't yet. It is a chart you'll go back to again and again all year, so be sure to have it displayed somewhere kids can see it and you can refer to it easily.*

SESSION 3: RETURNING TO A PAGE TO ADD MORE

ACTIVE ENGAGEMENT

Rally kids to look at their pieces and consider what they will add in their pictures and words.

"Now it's your turn, writers. I bet you can be the kind of writers who are like Joy Cowley. The kind of writers who say, 'What more can I show and tell? Try it now. Pull out your writing from yesterday." I gave the kids a few seconds to look at their work. "Can you add details around your object to show where your object is or even what is happening?

"Tell your partner what you will add to the page in your pictures and your words!" I listened in as students shared with one another. Then I said, "Jason says that he wants to draw his train in the store where he got it with his mom and write *store* and *mom*. And Giselle wants to draw and write about her doll at her birthday party and all of the friends who were there! They're telling more about where their special objects are and about what's going on."

LINK

Send children off, reminding them to add more to their writing to help their readers understand it even more.

"Writers, we've talked a lot about how you are going to help your readers know more by adding some more to each page. One way to show and tell more is to tell *where* something is and what's going on.

"People are going to be *dying* to read your writing and to learn about your special thing, so today, will you make sure that when you go back to your pages, you add more? For the first few minutes of writing time today, I'm going to 'close' the paper tray in our writing center so that we all try returning to the work we've already started." I hung a "Closed" sign on the paper tray. "Once we all work for a little, I'll open it up again!

"Now off you go! Add more to your writing to help your readers understand more!"

To keep lessons short, we suggest you share out what you hear students say, rather than calling on kids. This also allows you to shape kids' answers to be closer to what you are getting at. Saying what you heard gives all students another example of the kind of work you are asking them to do.

The goal of this lesson is to get children to add more to their work, but don't expect that they'll be able to do this for more than a few minutes. You may open up the writing center after five or six minutes and encourage kids to get started on a new piece if they are ready. They could write another page about their object or something they're wearing or something they brought to school.

---

14   SHOW AND TELL WRITING: FROM LABELS TO PATTERN BOOKS

CONFERRING AND SMALL-GROUP WORK

Creating Transfer between Isolated Phonics Work and Writing

WHEN A CHILD ISN'T LABELING HER PICTURES, you need to know why. Does that particular child know letters and sounds? If so, what's getting in her way? Does she have the phonemic awareness necessary to say the word slowly, segmenting the sounds? If she can break a word into constituent sounds and knows half her letters and sounds, then perhaps this is a child who needs to be encouraged to take risks. Perhaps she just needs you to be more firm that yes, she is expected to shift between drawing and writing.

But of course, this child may not be writing because she may hardly know any letters and sounds, or she may need help segmenting a word into its parts. Your first step is to recognize that it is a bit of a problem if the child isn't at least writing labels (correctly or incorrectly) during writing time. Once you've said to yourself, "I need to look into this," that research is easily conducted. Many teachers find it helpful to keep an alphabet sheet for each child, marking off when there is evidence that the child can recognize and name the uppercase and a lowercase letter, and can name the associated sound. The good thing is that you can recruit teaching assistants, student teachers, and others to help you conduct an assessment like this. For now, the important thing will be to do this with just the children who aren't writing.

Once you know the status of the class, you'll determine your next steps. What letters require extra attention for the whole class? Which students require lots of quick practice to get closer to the goal of all students knowing letters and sounds as soon as possible? Use this information as you conduct your conferences and small groups.

Sometimes students know their letters and sounds, but still don't seem to get words on the page. They need to learn to say words slowly and isolate phonemes. You might listen and coach into this process over and over again during conferences. Your process might sound like this:

- Ask the child, "What's a word we could say/write about this object?"
- Prompt the child to stretch out the sounds, with increasing scaffolding as needed:
  - "Say it slowly!"
  - "Try it again. Say it even more slowly and move your hand down your arm."
  - "Listen to me say it slowly. Now you try it."
  - "Let's try saying it slowly together."
- Prompt the child to find the corresponding letter.
  - "What letter makes that sound?"
  - "Does it sound like /c/ *cat* or /t/ *table*?"

As you do this with students, take note of what each child can do. Can the child say the word slowly on his or her own without you? You'll want to take special note to gather these students for more repeated practice in a small group, such as the following possibility.

MID-WORKSHOP TEACHING
Writers Push Themselves to Add Even More

"Writers, eyes up here." I waited until I had children's full attention. "You are doing hard work today—it's much easier to whip up a piece of writing, then to put it aside and say, 'Next,' and then whip up another piece, and another. But you are going back to yesterday's writing and adding more. Put it in front of you where you and your partner can see it. Will you silently point out to your partner the parts of your work that you added to today?"

I gave children a minute or two. "Now, writers, think what *else* can you add? Maybe you could add in what you like to do with your special treasure, or where you keep it in your house. Tell your partner what you're going to add!"

In a small group or table conferences, support students who need more practice with phonemic awareness by using Elkonin boxes.

If students have difficulty saying words slowly and isolating sounds, you'll want to strengthen this aspect of phonemic awareness. You might use Elkonin boxes, which help students segment words into individual sounds or phonemes. Elkonin boxes are a series of boxes, with each box representing one sound, or phoneme, in a word. To use Elkonin boxes, children can work alongside you to listen to words and move counters or tokens into a box for each sound. You might gather a small group or go to a table of students who need more practice and begin by saying, "I was thinking that we could get even more practice listening for sounds. We're going to listen today by saying a word and pushing counters into the boxes to show the sounds we say."

You can demonstrate each word, then have children try it with their own Elkonin boxes. You'll likely want to start with two-square Elkonin boxes and words with two phonemes (*it*, *in*, *on*). Once you've done repeated practice with two-phoneme words, on a different day, hand out Elkonin boxes with three squares and do a few words with three phonemes like *rug*, *cat*, and *box*. After students try this with words you've chosen, you can help students transfer this work into their own writing by having them try to segment words they want to write. A word they choose to write might have more than two or three phonemes. The point is that they are starting to hear letters and sounds.

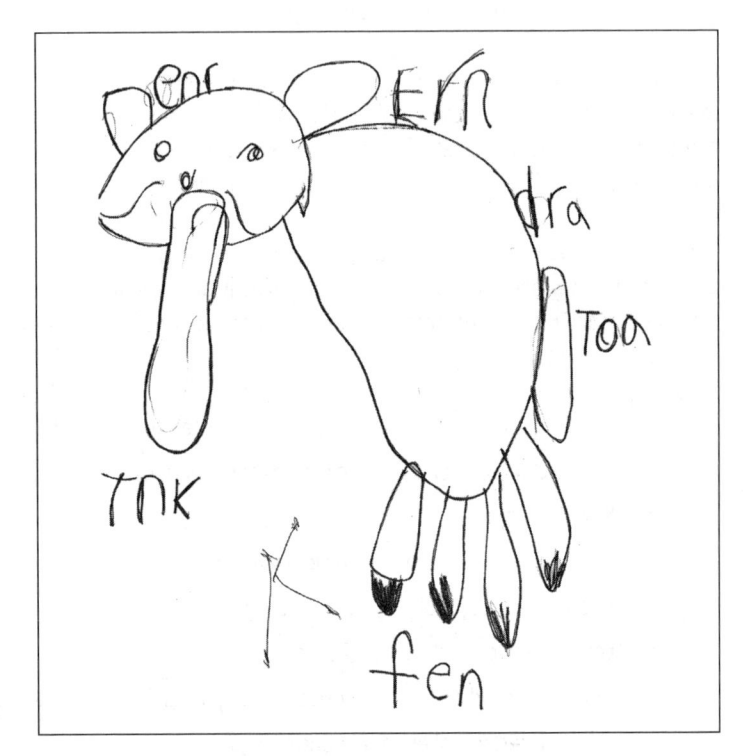

FIG. 3–1   Jeremiah went back and stretched to hear more sounds on his drawing of an elephant. (*Left to right, top to bottom*: ear, ear, body, tail, feet, trunk)

FIG. 3–2   Braedan stretched to hear more sounds on her cat drawing. (*Left to right, top to bottom*: ear, legs, feet, belly, mouth)

SHARE

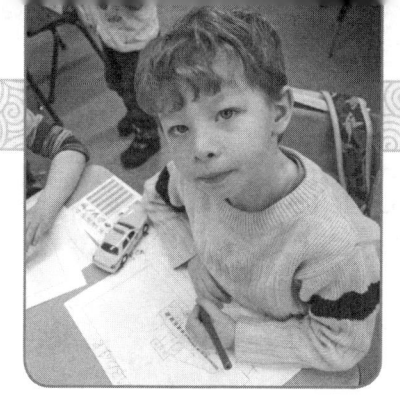

Supporting Writing Identities

Invite writers to talk about their writing work, naming what they tried or what they are proud of. Then, play a song to celebrate.

"Writers, look at your writing. When you stick with something for a while before going straight to the next thing, it can give you a feeling of 'I'm proud.'

"Will you notice what you did today that you are proud of? Put your finger on that part."

I waited, and once most had located a part, I said, "Tell each other about those parts. You might use words like, 'I worked hard to . . . ' or 'I'm proud that I . . . '

"I have a song to celebrate. Put your writing in the 'still working' or 'done' side of your folder and come to the meeting area." I pressed play on the online video of Will. I. Am's *Sesame Street* song "What I Am" and we danced along.

"You are all getting smarter! I bet you are proud! I'll hang up the words to this song, so we can sing it all the time."

SESSION 3: RETURNING TO A PAGE TO ADD MORE

Session 4

Writers Use Everything They Know to Spell Words and Don't Wait to Be Perfect

GETTING READY

- ✔ Be sure to have your tools out (alphabet chart, snap word collection, name wall) to use during this session, along with chart paper and markers to write words and do interactive writing (see Teaching and Share).

- ✔ Children will need their writing folders and a pen or pencil for the minilesson (see Active Engagement).

- ✔ Place mini alphabet charts on or in students' writing folders, if you haven't already (see Active Engagement).

- ✔ Display the "Brave Spellers" anchor chart with the first three Post-its (see Link).

- ✔ Bring mailing labels and small adhesive stars for small-group work (see Conferring and Small-Group Work).

- ✔ You may want to draw a picture of a familiar object like a teddy bear for small-group work (see Conferring and Small-Group Work).

- ✔ Add to the "Brave Spellers" anchor chart by writing interactively on Post-its with students. Display the completed chart in the classroom. You'll want to refer to it all year, and you'll add a new Post-it to it in Session 7 (see Share).

IN THIS SESSION

TODAY YOU'LL teach students that writers try their best to write words on the page, even if they know the words are not spelled exactly right. You will demonstrate how to spell words by using all the tools in the room—the name wall, the alphabet chart, and the snap word chart.

TODAY YOUR STUDENTS will continue to draw and write pages about their objects. Expect to see students labeling at least five words on each page and using tools like the alphabet chart and name chart.

MINILESSON

CONNECTION

Challenge writers to work hard at writing words, even though they know what they are writing might not look the way it is written in a book.

"Writers, congratulations! You've been working to put stuff on the page—even when it's tricky. One thing I heard you say is that the pictures aren't the only tricky part. The words have been tricky, too!

"Yesterday some of you came up to me after checking the snap word chart and asked, 'How do I write about my robot? *Robot* isn't on the chart.' And that was a wise question because . . . I have a secret. Listen up." I waited a second. "*Most* of the time, when you want to write something, the words won't be on a chart on the wall.

"You could always line up beside a teacher and say (and I made my voice into a pathetic needy whine), 'Help me, help me,' but there won't always be teachers beside you when you want to write."

18 SHOW AND TELL WRITING: FROM LABELS TO PATTERN BOOKS

✤ Name the teaching point.

"Today I want to teach you that it is really important for you to say, 'I'll just be brave. I'll use everything I know—my name, my friends' names, the alphabet—to spell as best I can.' If you do that every day, pretty soon you'll be able to write any word in the whole wide world."

TEACHING

Demonstrate being a brave writer. Show how writers use all the tools in the room—the name wall, the alphabet chart, labels up in the room—to help write all of the sounds they hear.

"You know that I am *much* older than you. And I've been spelling words since I was small. So I know a lot of words. But I'm going to pretend to be a five- or six-year-old right now and show you what you can do when you want to spell a word.

"I want to write some more words on my page about my bunny. One thing I want to write is that she is fuzzy. I know that I don't know exactly how to spell *fuzzy*. But if I don't try . . . I won't have that important word on my page. And if I don't try, I won't get better. So let me try to hear the sounds and write down the letters I know.

"Can you help me say the word slowly?" I slowly said *ffff-uuu-zzzzzzz-eeee*, sliding my right hand down my left arm.

"I think I hear some sounds! *Fffff*, that sounds like the picture of *fan* on our alphabet chart! I'll write down the letter *F*. Maybe I can hear more sounds." I slid my hand down my arm again. *Fuuuuzzzz. Zzzzz*. Hmm, . . . that's like the *Z* in Aliza's name. I'll write the letter *Z*. *Fuzzeeee Eeeee*. Like the letter *E*." I wrote it down.

I pointed and read the word I'd written, *Fze*, as *fuzzy*.

Debrief. Help students notice that your spelling isn't the same as book spelling and that you used a variety of tools to help you.

"Writers, I know that the way we spelled *fuzzy* isn't perfect, but did we try the best we could? Yes! Did we say the word slowly and listen to as many sounds as we could hear? Yes. We even heard the ending sounds, didn't we? *Fuzzeeee*.

"For the rest of your life, you will want to be the kind of person who is brave enough to do the best you can. When other kids get together to play basketball, if you wait until the day you can do things perfectly, you'll just sit on the bench, saying, 'No, thank you. I'm not going to play until I'm perfect.'

"You know what? You'll never be a good writer or a good basketball player if you just sit around and wait until the day you are perfect. Instead, you need to get started. You need to say, 'I'm not perfect, but I'll try.'"

This concept is one of the most essential to this unit. Without a strong sense of "Yes, I can," students will be less likely to attempt this challenging work. The "Brave Spellers" anchor chart you'll use during the share of this session will be especially important for illustrating this concept.

If you draw something different, we recommend you choose a word that not all kids know how to spell easily. Also, avoid words that don't follow conventional spelling patterns, like eye or ear. Demonstrate how you write down the salient sounds in the word.

FIG. 4–1 Teacher example with inventive spelling.

ACTIVE ENGAGEMENT

Recruit students to try spelling words on their own. Remind them to use strategies like saying words slowly and referring to the alphabet chart.

"Who's willing to give this a go? Who's brave enough to try doing some of your own writing?" Hands shot up. "So pull your work out of your folder. I put a little alphabet chart in your folder to help! Ready to get started right now? Point to something in your pictures—to anything—and say that word aloud. Then get started, writing it as best you can."

As writers worked, I coached. "I see you saying a word, then looking at the alphabet chart for the first sound. I'm seeing some of you singing the ABC song to find the letter you want. Such good work!"

LINK

Remind students that from now on, they will use all their tools and do their best at spelling words, even if it's not perfect.

"Writers, this is hard work. From now until the end of time we are going to not just say, 'Ehhh, that's good enough. I wrote the first sound, or I wrote one letter.' Now we are going to think, 'I'm going to do my very best, even if it's not perfect or if it doesn't look the same as it might in a book. I'm going to use all the tools in the room to help me try my very best.'

"Now I'm going to put up this 'Brave Spellers' anchor chart and these pictures to help us remember to be brave, use tools, and stretch out words." I put up the "Brave Spellers" anchor chart.

As students add more letters to their labels, keep in mind that they are likely to include the salient sounds first, the sounds they hear the most clearly. This may not always be the first and last sounds. It may be the medial sound.

Each day, you'll want to be sure children are using their alphabet chart and have it nearby. Do what works best—a table alphabet chart or individual charts pasted on the front of folders. The most important thing is that kids use the tool!

In the share, you'll add the words to the "Brave Spellers" anchor chart using interactive writing. You'll want to display the chart, so children can refer to it throughout this unit. You will add a new Post-it to this chart in Session 7.

SHOW AND TELL WRITING: FROM LABELS TO PATTERN BOOKS

CONFERRING AND SMALL-GROUP WORK

Supporting Reluctant Writers

TODAY YOU MAY WANT TO PAY SPECIAL ATTENTION to your more reluctant writers. They might be waiting to get started until you come to them, idly adding to their drawings or asking a friend to help them spell. To figure out what's stopping them, you may want to refer to the conferring in Session 3 for tips on how to assess young writers. You'll want to balance offering support with letting them productively struggle through getting words down on the page. See the small groups below for ideas on how to give them an extra boost.

In a small group, table conference, or one-to-one conference, support reluctant writers with special tools.

If a few students resist writing words, you may simply give them a new tool. You might ask a child to tell about the picture, and while listening, plop Post-its alongside objects in the picture that warrant a label. Or you might plop mailing labels in those spots, saying, "This is your mom? Right here, write *mom*." You can introduce these "special tools" in a small group or simply dip in and out of one-to-one conferences.

A small group or table conference can allow you to do this work with efficiency. "Writers, some of you seem nervous about adding words. Here are some special stickers to help you plan and write lots of words. Will you find one thing on your picture that you want to label and touch it? Good! Touch two or three other things that you want to label." As children are touching parts of their pictures, you may want to put mailing labels on those spots and encourage kids to write words on the labels. You'll want to coach students to say the words slowly and use their alphabet chart to match the sounds they hear with the letters. You may also use these labels to remind children to write from left to right. If you put a star on the left side of the label, that star will remind them where to start.

Support children with matching sounds and letters through interactive writing table groups.

When you convene an interactive writing group at a table, you might begin by asking students to help you with your writing (or say your neighbor needs help with her writing). You could then share a text in which you have already drawn a picture of a familiar object like a teddy bear. Channel students to help you point to parts you could label. As you work to write words, invite students to say the words slowly, segmenting the words and isolating the sounds. Recruit the children to help you find the letter that matches on the alphabet chart and share the pen with kids, so they also help write the letters. For example, you might share the pen for the first letter of the words *paw*, *tummy*, *nose*.

As you work together, you can use prompts like:

- "Say the word slowly. Catch the first sound. What sound did you hear?"
- "Move your hand down your arm as you say that word. *Beeeeaaaarrrr*." (Move your hand slowly from your shoulder to wrist, stretching out the word as you go.)

MID-WORKSHOP TEACHING
Celebrating Brave Attempts and Hard Work

"Writers, I am blown away by your bravery. There are writers in this room who didn't have any words on their papers yesterday, and today their papers are filled up with words. You should be so proud of how hard you have worked to get the letters and sounds down. When writers have worked hard and are super-proud, they share it with other people. Right now, will you point to a word on your paper that you worked really hard to write, and share it with you partner?" Kids turned to the person next to them and said, "I'm proud of this word, and this word."

"Wow! Such proud writers, give your partner a high-five for all that hard work! Now guess what? We can't stop there, we can keep going, writing even more words to teach our readers even more!"

- "Do you know what letter makes that sound? Let's check the alphabet chart."
- "Say the word again. What other sounds do you hear?"

After about three to five minutes of interactive writing, invite children to return to their writing. You might say, "Now it is your turn to put words on your pages. You can try doing what we just tried, and I'll coach you. Point and say the first word you want to try, and get going!" You can float from table to table today and the next, conducting quick bits of interactive writing.

Even as you focus in on tables, groups, or individuals who need more support, remember that your whole class could probably benefit from some encouragement to get a lot of words down on the page. As you move about the room, you might say:

- "Remember when you said you didn't know how to spell? Now you are spelling all on your own!"
- "Look at all you are doing to be brave and get letters down on the page. What did you do to help yourself?"
- "You didn't just write one word, you didn't just write two words, you wrote three words!"

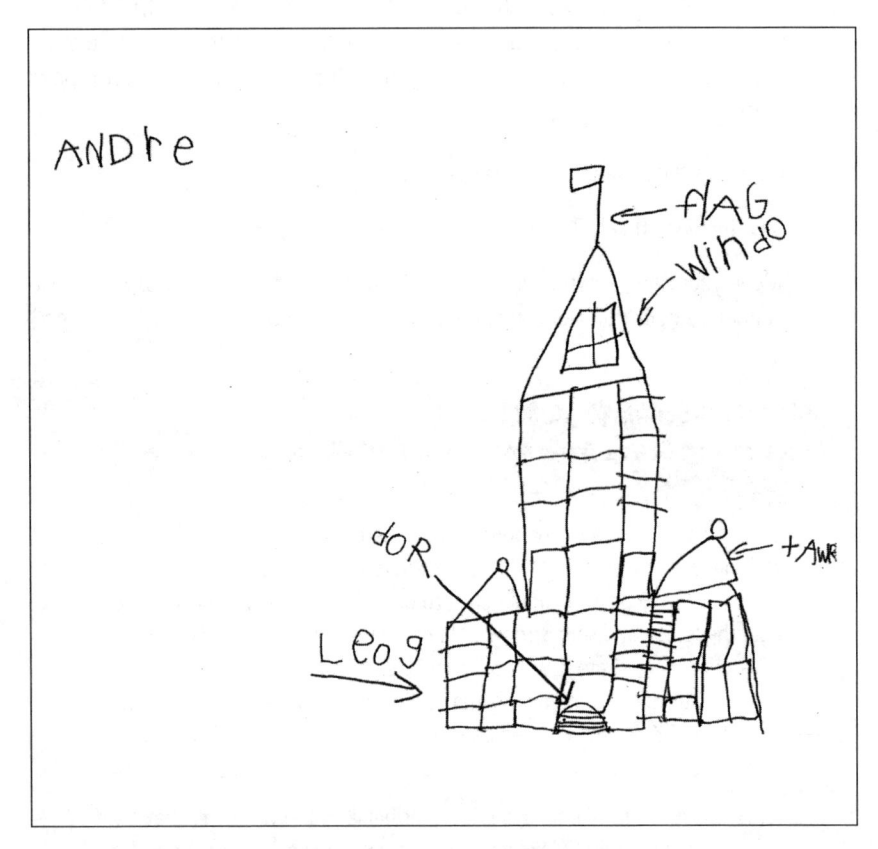

FIG. 4–2 Andre went back and added more words to his drawing of his Lego tower. (*Left to right, top to bottom*: Lego, door, flag, window, tower)

FIG. 4–3 Adele went back and added to her drawing of her Panda. (*Left to right, top to bottom*: eyes, ears, hands, feet, sailboat)

SHARE

Using Interactive Writing to Create a Class Spelling Chart

Use interactive writing to add words under each picture on the "Brave Spellers" anchor chart. Add the words: *Don't give up!*, *Use tools*, **and** *Stretch it out*.

"Writers, you spelled tricky words today! On the count of three, will you say some of the words you tried to write? One-two-three!" The class chimed in all at once. "Wow! Listen to all of those words. What brave spellers you are! Place your writing in your folders on the 'done' or 'still working' side and come to the meeting area."

"Let's add words to our 'Brave Spellers' chart to keep track of the ways that we can be brave spellers." I placed the chart on the easel.

"Will you take a minute to remember the ways that you worked to spell words today? Turn and tell your partner something you did to help yourself be a brave speller today." I listened in as students talked.

"I heard a few of you say that you didn't give up! Don't give up! That's important. Let's write that down under this picture here." I quickly wrote the first two words, *don't give*, and stopped at the word *up*. I invited children to help me hear the sounds and write the letters of this word, referencing the alphabet chart along with way.

I continued to write words for each picture on the chart, stopping to give the students opportunities for practice. As we wrote "use tools," the students practiced hearing and writing the first letters in *tools*. As we wrote, "stretch it out," they helped write the snap word *it* and the last letter in *out*.

"I know this is going to be an important chart. It will help us all remember how we can be the kind of brave spellers that we want to be. Let's read the chart together."

FIG. 4–4   A student adds to "Brave Spellers" chart.

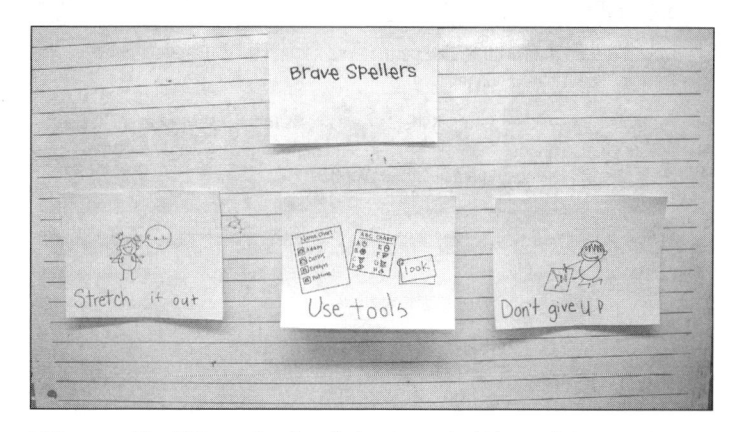

FIG. 4–5   Final "Brave Spellers" chart created through interactive writing.

Session 5

Writing Partners Can Help Each Other Celebrate and Add More

GETTING READY

- ✔ Get a box with student work from the beginning of year to use as a "time capsule" (see Connection).
- ✔ Children will need a piece of writing or their writing folders and a pen or pencils (see Connection, Active Engagement, Link).
- ✔ Bring out Mabel or another stuffed animal to play the part of your writing partner. Display your own earlier drawing and writing about the bunny and be ready to add to it (see Teaching).
- ✔ Introduce the "Writing Partners" anchor chart point by point (see Teaching and Active Engagement).
- ✔ Display a class chart with writing partners' names, indicating Partner 1 and Partner 2 (see Active Engagement).
- ✔ For table conferences, be sure students have access to the "Brave Spellers" anchor chart, alphabet chart, name chart, and high-frequency word cards or chart (see Conferring and Small-Group Work).

IN THIS SESSION

TODAY YOU'LL teach students that writing partners can help each other find ways to make their writing better. You will demonstrate how to work with a writing partner—put one book in the middle, read and talk, ask questions, and add more.

TODAY YOUR STUDENTS will return to previous writing to add more to their pictures and their words. Expect to see them talking with partners about their writing.

MINILESSON

CONNECTION

Celebrate how much writers have grown from the beginning of this unit by having them compare their writing from the first unit to their current writing.

"Was it just a few days ago when we talked about how much you had grown since the start of school? Remember, I told you that I bet your parents are saying 'slow down' because soon you'll outgrow all your school clothes. And we talked, then, about how you are growing as readers and as writers, too.

"Let's study how much you have grown. I have a special time capsule box of your writing from the very beginning of the year. It will let you see what you were like as writers in the first few days of school. Will you take out your writing from yesterday? I'm going to pass out this writing from the beginning of the year. Put the two pieces side by side."

I helped children pull off these directions. "Here is the important thing. Will you look at the writing you did at the start of this school year? Then look at the writing you did yesterday. Compare the two pieces and see if you have grown even more during this unit." I waited a minute for the children to note the differences.

SHOW AND TELL WRITING: FROM LABELS TO PATTERN BOOKS

"I'm wondering if some of you see drawings that have a lot more detail in them now? Hands up if you have that!" Children so signaled. "Hurrah! Stand up and take a bow," I said and led the class in clapping for them. "How many of you have more writing now?" Again, we cheered for those who so signaled.

"Writers, the way that your writing has gotten so good is that you have worked a long time on even just a page of writing. You have been willing to do work that is tricky and hard and important, and you've gone back to it more than once, thinking, 'I can make this even better.'"

I quickly collected students' work from the beginning of the year and put it back in the box. "I'm going to keep this work in here, so every so often we can pull it out and see how much we've grown!"

❖ **Name the teaching point.**

"Today I want to teach you that when you have done really good work, work that's the best of your life, that is not a time to say, 'I'm done' and stick your feet up on the table and relax. No way! When you've done your best, you go back to your best work and think, 'How can I make this even *better?*' Usually it helps to get a friend to help you."

TEACHING

Demonstrate how a partner can help you make your writing better by reading it and asking questions.

"I've brought a friend in to help me take my best writing and make it even better. I'm hoping you'll spy on what my friend and I do, then decide the steps we take so you can do the same thing. You ready?" I took out a stuffed elephant from behind the easel, Mabel!

"Watch carefully. I'll be the writer, and Mabel will be my writing partner."

> **Teacher:** Mabel, I'm done my writing about my bunny. Can you help me make it even better?
>
> **Mabel:** I'd love to! Would it be good if I read your writing, then ask you some questions so you can tell me more, then put more on the page?
>
> **Teacher:** Yes!

I put Mabel close to the page to "read the writing"—a picture of the rabbit with half a dozen one-word labels. Mabel "whispered" to the class: "Can you help me think of some good questions we could ask to get your teacher saying more? What would be good?"

I gave the class a moment to think and then talk with a partner. Mabel (and I) listened in.

> **Mabel:** Wow, I heard a lot of good questions! "Where do you keep the rabbit?" "Do you have others?" "What does she do?"

If this feels like too much to do logistically, you might simply show some student work from the beginning of the year next to work from the previous session under the document camera and ask students to notice the growth.

Instead of keeping the writing from the beginning of the year in a box, some teachers choose to display it on a bulletin board with the title, "Look How We've Grown." Then teachers can place students' most recent writing next to their writing from the beginning of the year to celebrate the growth they have made.

If you are using the Units of Study in Phonics for kindergarten, you will be familiar with Mabel, a stuffed elephant mascot. She appears often across the phonics units, helping kids to learn their letters, sounds, and high-frequency words. If you aren't teaching the Units of Study in Phonics, you can substitute any stuffed animal or puppet that's familiar to your students.

If you have a class with some English language learners, you might reference familiar charts to remind students of questions they could ask. For instance, you might create a chart with question stems. This way, students have ideas for the kinds of questions they could ask.

Teacher: Hmm, . . . well, I keep her on my bed next to my pillow! Should I add that into my drawing?

I helped Mabel nod.

I quickly added my bed and pillow, drawing an arrow to the spot where the rabbit was kept. I even quickly added the words *my*, *bed*, and *pillow*.

Debrief in a way that is transferable.

"Did you see what Mabel and I did? Let's see if we did all the things that writing partners do. I'm going to hang up this chart as we talk to make sure we didn't forget anything." I hung up the title Post-it "Writing Partners." "Will you say 'yes' if you saw Mabel and me do these things?"

I pulled the first Post-it off the pack and read, "Put one book in the middle." Kids chimed in, "Yes, you did!" I high-fived Mabel. I pulled the next one, "Read and talk." "Yes, we did that, too!" I double high-fived Mabel. "Next one, let's see!" I read, "Ask questions." "Yay, we did that, too!" I low-fived Mabel. "Last one, 'Add more.' Yeah, we did all of it!" I gave Mabel a hug.

ACTIVE ENGAGEMENT

Partners read and talk, ask questions, and add more to their drawing and writing.

"Partners, will you try talking in a similar way? Look at the 'Writing Partners' chart that I've made," I said, gesturing toward the anchor chart.

"From now on, some of you will be Partner 1 and some of you will be Partner 2. Partner 2, will you start? Partner 2, put your book in the middle. Show your picture and your words. Partner 2, will you look at the picture and ask some questions to help them add even more to their drawing and to the words?"

I floated around, listening in to partnerships, encouraging them to check the chart to make sure they had one piece in the middle, they were asking questions, and they were adding more.

LINK

Encourage writers to make a plan for how they will write more. Remind them that they can use their partners throughout writing workshop.

"Writers, come back together, and quickly whisper to yourself what your plan is when you go back to your writing spots. What will you add to your picture and your words?

"Writers, if you get stuck and can't think about what else you can write, ask your partner for help so you can go go go! Your partner is there to help you say more."

As you coach into partnerships, try to get the partners talking to each other rather than you. One way you can do this is by whispering in one partner's ear to get them to ask questions of the other person. You might whisper to one partner, "Ask him where they are" or "Ask her who that is."

CONFERRING AND SMALL-GROUP WORK

Predictable, Quick Interventions to Keep the Whole Class Writing Up a Storm!

Offer compliments that build your students' identities as writers.

- "You're not just teaching with pictures. I see you're also labeling. You are so much like _____ (mentor author)! All these words will really help your reader learn a lot! Is there another page you're going to try this on?"

- "I notice that you have your alphabet chart out to help you get all those words down on your paper. What a brave speller you are! I can't wait to see all the words you're going to write!"

- "Wow, you added to your pictures and words, and then decided you were ready to get started on a new piece *and* you didn't even need a reminder! Way to be the boss of your writing! I can't wait to see your next page!"

Encourage partners to help each other add more.

For students who are struggling with coming up with words to write, you might remind them of today's minilesson and have them turn to a partner for help. Say to two students sitting next to each other, "I wonder if your partner could help you come up with some words you could write down. Put your paper in the middle, point to your picture, and say some things you see." If they don't do anything, prompt the partner to help. "Juan, do you see anything that Jessica can label?" You might need to whisper in to the partner to get them to point to the picture and say, "What's that?" Stay with them for a few rounds, until the student has a few ideas to write about. Then prompt them to write the new ideas down.

Conduct table conferences to support students with using tools to write words.

As you conduct table conferences, take note of students' writing. You might notice some students appealing for help spelling unfamiliar words. You might notice other students omitting sounds in their labels or failing to spell high-frequency words correctly.

Coach those students to use the spelling tools you've introduced. "Writers, I see you've added a lot to your drawings, and you're ready to write more words. Remember, you've got lots of tools that can help you." I pointed to the "Brave Spellers" anchor chart. "You can use the alphabet chart, the name chart, and your snap word collection to help you spell words. It can help to think, 'Is this a word that I need to stretch out and hear the sounds? Or is this a snap word?' Right now, look at a page where you have a lot of drawing. Think about the words you want to write and use tools to write them. I'll help you as you go."

Ensure all students have started, then use familiar, lean prompts to coach each student and direct them to the tools that will best help them.

To support decision making:

- "What words do you want to write? Where will you write them?"

- "Is that a word to stretch or is it a snap word?"

MID-WORKSHOP TEACHING

Preparing a Piece for the Museum Share

"Writers, in just a few minutes, you are going to celebrate and share your work. Will you choose your best page, the page that you want to share with the whole class today? Close your writing folder and put that page on top. Now, take a few minutes to make your writing extra strong. Reread your writing. Put your finger under each word. Listen for the sounds you hear. Did you write all those sounds? If you hear any sounds that are missing, add them into your writing right now. Then, check the next word. Once you've checked all your words, see if there are other words you can add to your writing. Get to it. There's no time to waste!"

SESSION 5: WRITING PARTNERS CAN HELP EACH OTHER CELEBRATE AND ADD MORE

To support spelling work:

- "Say the word slowly. Listen for the sounds."
- "Look at the alphabet chart."
- "Is there a name that starts with that sound?"
- "Try to hear the first/next/last sound."
- "Does it sound like /s/ in the word *sun* or like /f/ in *fan*?" (Reference the pictures from the alphabet chart.)

To support high-frequency word work:

- "That's a snap word!"
- "Look at your snap word collection and say the letters."
- "Write it and say the letters."
- "Check it. Were you right?"

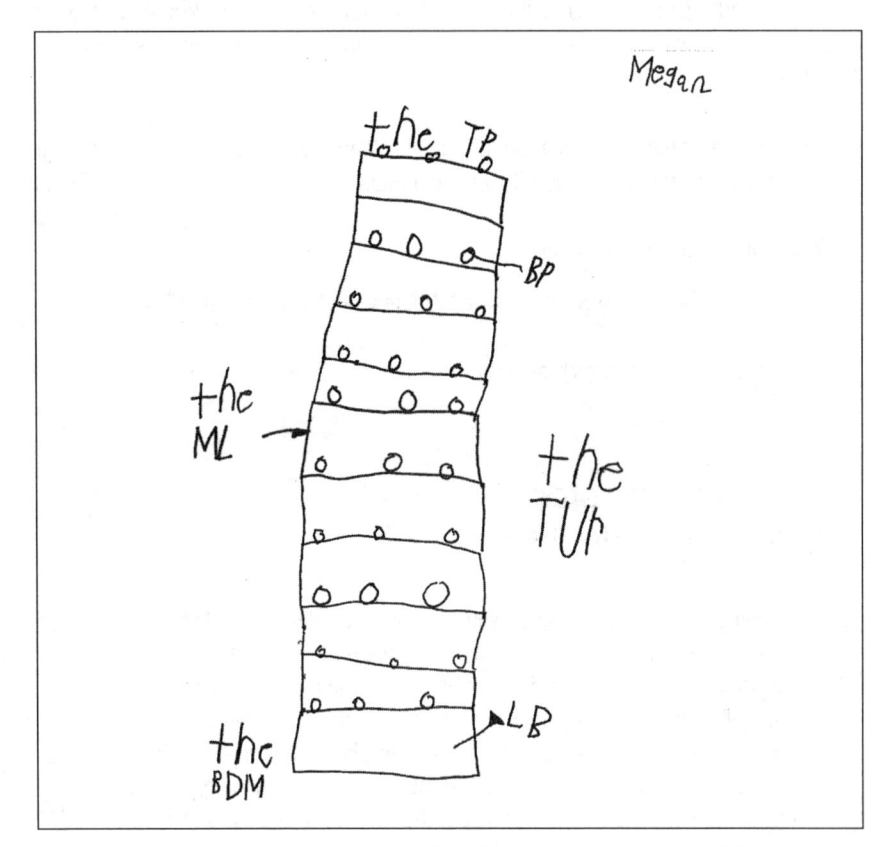

FIG. 5–1   Megan went back and added the high-frequency word *the* to her drawing of a tower. (*Clockwise from top*: the top, bump, the tower, blue, the bottom, the middle)

FIG. 5–2   Selena went back and added *my* to her words. (*Left to right, top to bottom*: smoke, car, windows, my car, my racecar, wheel, wheel)

SHOW AND TELL WRITING: FROM LABELS TO PATTERN BOOKS

SHARE

Celebrating with a Show-and-Tell Museum Walk

Engage students in a museum walk with their show-and-tell objects out on their desks and their writing next to it.

"Writers! Stop what you're doing and look up! Today is going to be a special share. Today is the day that we are going to really show *and* tell, not just about our special objects but also about our writing! Listen carefully. First, put your writing and your special object out on your desk. Now take your folder and put it away. Leave only your writing and your object out." I looked around the room to see that everyone had followed directions. "Okay, now come to the rug so I can tell you how this will go."

"Put a thumb on your knee if you've ever been to a museum." A few kids had thumbs on their knees. I continued, "Today, we are going to celebrate our work by making our classroom into a museum! We will walk around and look and learn and admire all of the writing in our room.

"This is how people at museums act. Ready? Now watch me." I stood up, my hands clasped behind my back. I leaned over to look closely at some of the writing. In an exaggerated, serious voice, I said, "Wow, this person wrote a lot of words!" Then I scratched my chin and said, "Wow, they must really love robots!"

"Did you see how I carefully walked around the room? I didn't touch anything, I just looked and said what I noticed."

"Are you ready to try it?" Kids nodded. "Okay, get into the museum frame of mind. We have to be serious at the museum." Kids started walking around with their hands behind their backs, bending over, scratching their chins, and commenting and admiring work they were looking at.

SESSION 5: WRITING PARTNERS CAN HELP EACH OTHER CELEBRATE AND ADD MORE

BEND II Writing Show-and-Tell Books

Session 6

Writers Write Show-and-Tell Books about Important Places

IN THIS SESSION

TODAY YOU'LL teach students that writers can tell about topics, like important places and things, by thinking about the parts of the topic and drawing and writing about them on pages in a book.

TODAY YOUR STUDENTS will write books about places that are important to them. Expect to see students using four-page booklets (cover and three pages), filling the pages up with drawings, and writing about five labels per page.

GETTING READY

- Before class, prepare a good supply of four-page booklets, each with a cover and three pages for writing, for you and your students to use during this session. Paper samples for booklets are on the online resources.
- Display "To Write a Show-and-Tell Book" anchor chart (see Link).
- Be ready to hand out mini-copies of a chart titled "Get an Idea" to kids in your small group (see Conferring and Small-Group Work).

MINILESSON

CONNECTION

To create a drumroll for this new bend, tell a story about a child sharing about a place he or she visited. Then invite writers to think about places that they could show and tell others about in a book.

"Writers, this morning Anna told me about visiting her grandma's house over the weekend, and I suggested she write about that for show and tell. You know what she did? She laughed at me. She really did. She just started saying, 'Ha ha ha, that is so funny.'

"But I was serious, so I asked her why she thought I was being funny. She said she couldn't possibly bring her grandma's house to school! She couldn't put her grandma's house in a bag and set her grandma's house on the corner of her desk. It wouldn't fit.

"That got me thinking. None of us can bring all of the things that we care the most about to school in a bag. We can't always put the people and the pets and the toys we love beside us as we write. But should that stop us from writing about those things? No way.

"So I thought we'd start some new work today. For the next week or so, we might show and tell about important things that are tricky or too big to bring to school. Maybe, for starts, we all borrow Anna's idea and think about whether we could use our drawing and our writing to capture the places that matter to us. We could write about places like our apartments and houses, our school, the park you love to go to, a friend's house, or even the zoo.

"Think right now about the places that matter to you. Do you have some in mind? Tell your partner what those places are." I listened in and coached writers. I also voiced over some of the ideas I was hearing. "Wow! The grocery store! The mall! Your home! The place where you go bowling!"

"The thing is, when you want to tell a lot, one page can't hold it all. You need a book."

❖ **Name the teaching point.**

"Today I want to teach you that if you want to write about a huge topic, it often helps to write a whole book on that topic. And before you write, you can think, 'What are the parts of this topic?' and then you draw and write one part on one page and another part on another page."

TEACHING

Demonstrate how to plan a book by thinking about the parts of the topic. Recruit children to think with you as you consider the parts.

"Some kids find this hard, so let's practice it. I think it's hard to think about the *parts* to something. Will you help me think about the parts?"

I took out a blank booklet to model with and said, "Let's write a book to tell about an important place for all of us—the classroom." I wrote "The Classroom" on the cover. "Now I need to ask, 'What are the parts of this topic, the classroom?' Think and tell your partner what the parts could be."

After a moment of talking, I called the class together and continued. "The first part could be the library. Let me draw and write that part on the first page. I'll draw the shelves and the book bins and the bean bags and the rug." After drawing, I quickly labeled "shelves," "book bins."

I turned to the next page in the booklet. "Let's keep going. Think: What could the next part be?" I paused to give children a bit of thinking time. "I'm thinking the next part could be the tables and chairs. Let me draw and write that part, too." I drew tables and chairs and labeled "tables" and "chairs."

"If we had time, we could think of and draw and label more parts, right? What other parts could go on different pages in our book?" Soon the class had generated an idea or two for the other pages.

Do not fear if your students don't have ideas yet. Instead of asking them to turn and talk, you can give more examples of things they could write about. Choose things that are important to them—restaurants you know they like, places they like to visit.

You'll notice that we are not spending time on showing kids how we stretch out words to write them. Our goal in this minilesson is to show the whole writing process: idea generation, planning, and writing. You will be teaching into stretching words out during small groups and later sessions.

ACTIVE ENGAGEMENT

Invite children to practice thinking and talking about the parts of another topic that could go in a book.

"Let's practice thinking about another topic together. You all know a lot about the playground. Will you think about the parts of the playground that could go in a book? Turn and talk. Work together to think about the parts of the topic! See if you can think about three parts!"

After a minute I said, "Time's up. I heard lots of ideas for different parts of the topic. The slide, the swings, the sandbox!"

LINK

Distribute four-page booklets and coach students to begin their books in the meeting area.

"Before you leave this meeting area, I'm going to give you a book with a cover and three pages. Will you decide what you will write about? It should be a place you love. It can absolutely be this classroom, or our playground, or our school, but it can also be your church, or the mall, or your house, or your bedroom.

"Then will you tell your partner what the parts of your book will be?"

Once children had done that, I unveiled a new anchor chart. "Writers, any time you want to write and show and tell something in a book, you can think of an idea, tell the parts, and then you can draw and write the parts! Off you go!"

Your coaching here sets students up to write four-page books, with a cover and three pages for writing. This will allow students to write about several parts of their topic. Certainly students could also write longer books.

Here's another place where it's important to give students examples of what they could write about. Don't be discouraged if they all choose the same topic as you for this first book—this is one way writers try out writing. The more examples you give, the more likely it is that students will choose different topics.

Passing out new paper at the start of a bend is always tricky. Alternatively, you may choose to place a stack of booklets on each table.

SESSION 6: WRITERS WRITE SHOW-AND-TELL BOOKS ABOUT IMPORTANT PLACES

CONFERRING AND SMALL-GROUP WORK

Building Momentum for the New Work and Supporting Idea Generation

TODAY, EXPECT YOUR KIDS WILL EACH WRITE an entire three-page book, four pages including a cover. During this bend, kids will write about a book a day, alternating with days for revision. The start of a new bend is a time to build excitement around new writing work, support purpose, and bolster students' stamina. One way to do this is by moving around the room, voicing over the work you expect to be seeing. You might walk around the classroom looking over students' shoulders, taking special note of the following categories and giving general directions to kids, reminding them to do the work you'd like to see.

Use voiceovers to promote student practice.

To support drawing:

- "Remember to use your whole page to draw. Make your drawings big enough so you can add details!"
- "Draw part by part. Do the best you can!"
- "Remember to draw all the tiny details."

To support writing words:

- "Point around the page. Say a word and write a word."
- "Say the word slowly and use the alphabet chart or the name chart to help you."
- "Write a word the best you can and then go on to the next."

To support growth mind-set:

- "You used to just hear one sound and write down one letter. Now look at all the sounds and letters you are hearing!"
- "You are working hard and trying new things. You must be proud."
- "You didn't just write one word, or two words, you wrote *lots* of words!"

To support the writing process:

- "I bet you are thinking about a place you love or a place you go. It could be your house, the park, the store . . ."
- "Remember to write about a different part on every page. What part will be on the page you're making?"
- "Wow, you got started on a new piece all on your own! Way to be the boss of your writing!"

Because you've moved from having students write about objects that are in front of them to writing about things from their memory, some students may have extra trouble

---

MID-WORKSHOP TEACHING **Picturing Our Topics in Our Minds to Show Them on the Page**

"Writers, I want you to remember that once you have something you want to write about, especially something that you can't bring in and set on your desk, it helps to really picture it, so you can remember all the details. Sometimes, you might close your eyes, try to see what you want to make in your head, and then think, 'How could I put this on the page?'

"Will you try this now? What's the next thing you're going to write about? Give a thumbs up when you know. Now close your eyes. Try to see that thing in your head. What does it look like? Zoom in close. Turn it over in your mind. Can you picture it? Now pick up your pen and draw it on the page."

---

34   SHOW AND TELL WRITING: FROM LABELS TO PATTERN BOOKS

in coming up with ideas. If you see this happening to more than one student, you may convene a small group to help kids generate ideas for multiple books.

In a small group, support students in generating ideas for multiple books.

Begin this group by explaining why you've gathered students together and naming your teaching point. "Writers, it can be tricky to get ideas for writing. It helps to ask, 'Where do I go a lot?' Right now, will you tell me one place you go to a lot. Maybe that is a place you went last weekend or maybe last night."

You could look at one child, expectantly. If he is silent and just shrugs, ask him, "Did you go to your kitchen?" If he nods, then say, "Whoa! Great idea, Miguel. I can imagine you might have a part that is the sink and another part where food is kept."

I tried a similar tack with another child. "Where did you go last weekend, Sara? Did you go to any stores? Or did you do something with a friend? Where? On your front stoop! Whoa. Maybe you'll write about the different people or things you saw from your stoop.

"So writers, do you see that in just a jiffy, you already thought of a few good places you could write about. Right now, tell each other one *more* place you could write about. I'm going to give you each a few blank books. I'll help you write the name of one place on one cover and write another place on another cover. That way you can hang onto your ideas for your books."

As students get started, you might coach in. Prompt kids using phrases like:

- "Think about places you go a lot . . . "
- "Do you want to take a look at some other kids' ideas?"
- "You got one idea, now try to get another!"
- "What an idea! How will the parts of your book go?"

Leave a mini "Get an Idea" chart with this group to help them remember how to get ideas.

SESSION 6: WRITERS WRITE SHOW-AND-TELL BOOKS ABOUT IMPORTANT PLACES

SHARE

Talking and Telling to Get Ready for Writing More Books

Invite writers to think about the next books that they will write and how the parts of those books will go. Let children know that in addition to writing about places, they can also write about important things.

"Writers, when I point to you with my magic wand, will you say the topic you wrote today? Say it out loud and proud!" I pointed to a few kids and they called out, "The grocery store!" "My house!" "My after school program!"

I said, "Wow! What important topics to show and tell about! You are probably just about ready to start a new book, so let's get some more ideas. Think about an important place—like where you take dance lessons—or maybe even an important thing like the subway or your mom's jewelry box. What important place or thing will you write your next book about? What will the parts be? Turn and tell someone nearby." I listened in as children shared some of their next topics.

Afterward, I reminded them to choose which side of their folder to place their writing in.

Session 7

Writers Make Time for Drawing *and* Writing

IN THIS SESSION

TODAY YOU'LL teach students that writers make time for writing words. For a day or two, it may help to set aside time for writing words so that children remember to do this.

TODAY SOME STUDENTS will begin by finishing writing books from the previous session, and others will start writing new books. Expect most writers to be working on their second or third book by the end of today's workshop, beginning a new book whenever they are ready. During writing time, expect to see students writing several one- and two-word labels on their pictures.

GETTING READY

- Children will need their writing folders and pens for the minilesson (see Active Engagement).
- Bring an oven timer, clock, or other timing/alarm device, such as a smart phone or tablet (see Active Engagement and Mid-Workshop Teaching).
- Display and add to the "Brave Spellers" anchor chart from Session 4 (see Teaching and Link).
- Be sure children can see the class alphabet chart, name chart, and snap word chart as they write (see Active Engagement, Link, and Mid-Workshop Teaching).
- Display the "Writing Partners" anchor chart (see Share).

MINILESSON

CONNECTION

Explain that just like reading workshop has two parts—partner time and private time—you think writing workshop could also have parts—drawing time and writing time.

"Writers, I have an idea for writing workshop, and it is actually an idea I got from the *reading* workshop! You know how one part of reading time is private reading time, and another part is partner reading time?

"My idea is that during writing workshop, there should be parts as well. One part can be for drawing—and the other, for writing. I'm suggesting this because even though this is writing time, you know what I have noticed? Some of you get so busy making your drawings that . . . you won't believe this . . . you *forget* to write!

"What I want to teach you today is pretty obvious. It's one of those things that makes you say, 'Duh!' You ready?"

❖ **Name the teaching point.**

"Today I want to teach you that during writing time, you . . . write!"

TEACHING

Explain that people often use reminders to remember the most important things. Challenge students to take ownership during writing workshop by setting reminders for themselves.

"The important thing to know is that in life, when I find I am forgetting to do something, I come up with reminders so that I don't forget anymore. Like in my family, we need a reminder to wake up in the morning. Honest. If we didn't have a reminder, we'd sometimes sleep right past the bus. So I set an alarm clock to ring at the time when I want to wake up.

"I'm thinking that in this class, many of you need reminders to shift from drawing to writing, so let's set our alarm. For now, when you leave the minilesson, try drawing for a little while, and then have the alarm tell you, 'Time to write.'

"But writers, you might also need other reminders. Like you might need reminders that help you so that when you spell, you put in a *lot* of letters because you use the alphabet." I pointed toward the "Brave Spellers" anchor chart. "Let's read this for other reminders."

ACTIVE ENGAGEMENT

Channel students to shift from drawing time to writing time right there on the rug with you.

"Ready to try this? Take out your folders and your pens and put them on your lap. You're going to practice moving from drawing time to writing time. I'll set our special alarm." I pulled out the oven timer I brought from my kitchen and put one minute on the clock. "When I hit 'go,' it's going to be drawing time.

"Take out a book from your folder." I gave kids a few seconds to think, and then I drumrolled my hands on my lap. "Now start drawing!" I hit "start" on the timer. I moved around and coached students as they worked on their drawings.

After a minute, the alarm went off. Most students stopped drawing and looked up at me. "The alarm went off! We know what that means." "Writing time!" the class responded.

"When you start writing time, think about whether you need some tools near you to help you write words. Tell your partner what will help you." After writers talked for a moment, I called them back. "Yes, I hear you saying that the alphabet chart and the name chart will be helpful during your writing time. And the snap word chart, too! Good thinking! Don't forget to use those tools. Go ahead and start your writing time!"

You may recall that you made this chart interactively with your students in the Session 4 share. In the link, you'll add a new strategy to this chart.

You might expect students to add one or two things to their drawings during this time.

Expect children will write one or two words during this quick rehearsal—but the point will have been made.

I coached writers as they began working. "Look at you getting those words down!" "Wow, Oscar used his alphabet chart to help him!" "Keep going, try to get more letters, more words!" "Such brave spellers!" "Some people are using the snap word chart to help them!" I gave kids about a minute to write.

LINK

Restate the teaching point. Encourage students to use all the reminders they need to help themselves write the best they can. Send them off to begin their drawing time.

"To help you remember to both draw *and* write today, let's continue to set the alarm! After some time for drawing, the alarm will go off. Instead of jumping out of bed, you can jump into your writing. We're going to add another reminder to our 'Brave Spellers' anchor chart." I added the Post-it that said, "Write lots of words." "And you have yourself—you're the one who can push yourself to do your best. To say, 'Yes! I can do this. I can keep going.'

"It's time to go back to your seats to start . . . drawing time! Remember, when the alarm goes off it's time for . . . " I paused to let kids call out, "Writing time!"

"Now off you go!"

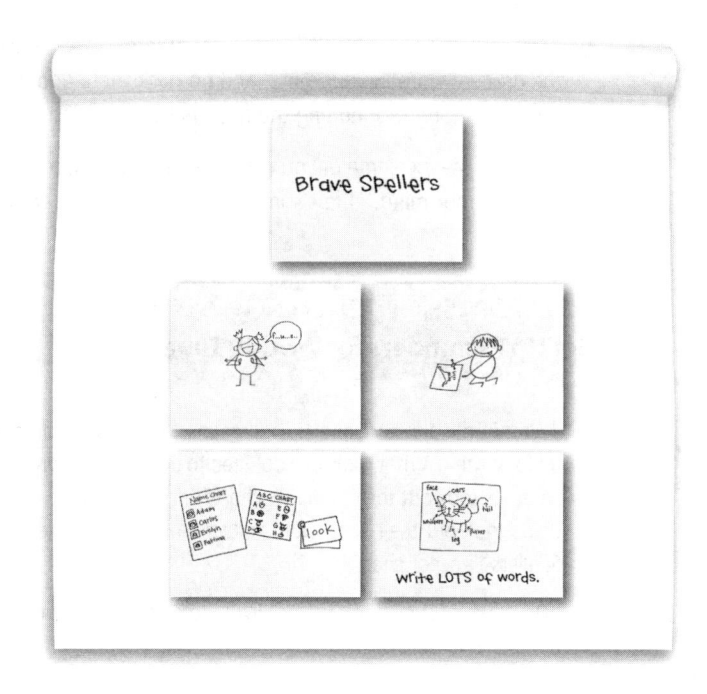

Use your knowledge of your students to decide how much to nudge them to write instead of draw. You might ask them what their plan is for writing words. Check in frequently to see that they are both drawing and writing.

SESSION 7: WRITERS MAKE TIME FOR DRAWING *AND* WRITING

39

CONFERRING AND SMALL-GROUP WORK

Supporting Children as They Move through the Writing Process

Help students move through the writing process, being sure they are adding pictures *and* words.

You might have questions like, "What if a child is ready to start planning and drawing a new book—and it's writing time?" or "What if the child is ready to write words and it is still drawing time?" We hope that the bigger message comes across to you. Kids need reminders to try to write words if they are not yet writing them.

For many, this will mean going back and adding words to pictures they've already drawn. Some kids may have filled up pages with labels and be ready to start a new page or piece. If so, they'd have to get a new page and draw a picture to have something to label. It's okay if drawing happens during writing time. Helping students know when to start a new book and when to revise and add more, while maintaining student choice and autonomy, is tricky. You can convey that kids are in charge of their writing—and also that you fully expect they'll find many ways to make their writing better.

To guide your thinking on when a child's work is "done," here's a rule of thumb. For kids working at benchmark levels, they would probably have five to six labels on each page of their writing and would be expected to write several pages a day. When you look at a student's paper, you might say, "You're off to a good start with those two labels. What else will you label on this page?" If a child has five labels, you might say, "You're the boss of your writing, so you need to decide if you're done with this page or if you want to move to another page." Once a child is writing with many of the salient sounds in a word, you will want to channel the child to write sentences, not just labels.

In table conferences, remind students to use all they know to make their writing the best it can be.

To support the work of writing words, you will probably move around the room, quickly conducting table conferences. Table conferences often follow a predictable structure.

To start, you'll often pull up to a table and observe the work children are doing, taking note of something beautiful or useful that one child is doing that all children would benefit from doing, too. You might say, "Writers, can I pause you for a moment?" Share out this work in a transferable way, using the child's example as a mentor text. After sharing the example, nudge all the students to try the work. Following, you'll find some predictable table conferences that will especially pay off at this point in the unit.

If you see a student drawing with lots of details, you might say:

- "Writers, Kira has done something writerly. She added flowers that are sold at the grocery store. What a detail!"
- "Kira, did you ask yourself, 'What else is there at my place?' Then did you picture the grocery store in your mind, and go back there and look things over? Is that how you thought of adding the flowers? Good going."
- "Writers, maybe some of you can try Kira's technique now. Get a picture of your place in your mind." I left some silence. "Now look around. What do you see?

MID-WORKSHOP TEACHING
Set Up Reminders for Writing Time

"Writers, the alarm went off! That means it's time for writing! Get yourself set up for writing. What tools do you need to do your best writing?" I watched as students took out their alphabet charts or set their name charts up. Some students took out their snap word collection baggies. Some studied the "Brave Spellers" anchor chart.

"Don't wait for me, get writing! Write lots of words! I can't wait to read and admire your words."

Look for teeny details that other people didn't even notice. You see something? Thumbs up if you do."

- "Okay now, add that to your drawing. Go!"

If you see a student showing and telling different parts of the topic across pages, you might say:

- "Can I show you the parts of Elliot's book? He is writing about the store and thought about all the parts of the store. On this page, he put the place where people pay, and on this page, he put the outside with carts and plants."

- "Writers, can some of you be like Elliot? Will you think about other parts of your place that you could write another page about? Tell the person next to you what part you'll write about on your next page."

If you see a student who not only draws pictures, but also writes words, you might say:

- "Let's look at Sarah's book. I can see the pictures and I can read the words. Let's point and read together. Wow! We can learn so much from Sarah's book because she drew pictures *and* wrote words."

- "Writers, remember that you can draw pictures and write words, too! Will you point around your picture and say a word you could write? Do your best to write it now. Have your alphabet chart out if you need it!"

If you see a student who is finishing a book and ready to start a new book, you might say:

- "Dori finished a whole book already! She drew lots of pictures and wrote lots of words. She taught different things on every page. Now she's ready to write a new book. She thought of another place she loves a lot, Chuck E. Cheese!"

- "Writers, when you are done, what book will you write next? Turn and tell your partner. You could say, 'In my next book, I'll write about . . .'"

FIG. 7–1 Julie's writing about her house. (*Top to bottom, left to right*: Page 1 In my room, dresser, my fan, teddy, me, tall bed; Page 2 kitchen, table, food floor)

SESSION 7: WRITERS MAKE TIME FOR DRAWING AND WRITING

SHARE

Showing and Telling with Partners

Emphasize that now that children are writing booklets, writing partners can talk and ask questions after every page. Recruit one student to show and tell his writing while the class serves as his writing partners.

"Writers, lots of you wrote a whole book today. Some of you wrote even more. You've got so much to show and tell about! Bring one of your books and a pen to the meeting area now. Sit next to your partner so you can share all about your special place.

"Showing and telling is a little different when you have long books! Writing partners don't wait until the end of the whole book to talk and ask questions. Instead, they talk and ask questions along the way, since each page is about a different part of the topic. Let's try this together." I called Jonah to the front of the room. "Jonah is going to share his book about a place that's super-special to him, and we'll be his writing partners. We will talk and ask questions after he reads each page."

Jonah read his book about the train station, and I called on a few students to comment and ask questions after he shared each page. We coached Jonah to add a label to one of his pages.

Invite partners to share and remind them of the "Writing Partners" anchor chart. Coach partners as they work together, making sure that one book is in the middle.

"Are you ready to show and tell about the important places you wrote about, the ones that are too big to fit on your desks? Use the 'Writing Partners' tips to help you." I gestured toward the chart. "Just like you do in reading workshop, put one book in the middle. Then you read your book to your partner. You can read and talk. You might even have more details you can add to the page. Then turn and share the next page. Partner 1 will go first today. Get started showing and telling!"

Session 8

Writers and Illustrators Make Decisions

IN THIS SESSION

TODAY YOU'LL teach students that writers make decisions about the ways they put their pictures and words on the page. You'll demonstrate by showing students how you study a page, thinking aloud about the way the pictures and the words are laid out—and how you might try these ways with the class book.

TODAY YOUR STUDENTS will continue to make books about places, now thinking about how they will place the pictures and the words on the pages. Expect to see kids trying out new page layouts as they draw and write.

GETTING READY

- Before class, choose a book with lots of pictures and labels so you can show a page to the class. We use *The Ultimate Book of Vehicles: From Around the World* by Anne-Sophie Baumann and Didier Balicevic (see Teaching).
- Find another book that has pages or spreads with one large picture and sentences. We use *On the Go* by Roger Priddy (see Active Engagement).
- Be ready to demonstrate drawing and writing on a new page in the class book (see Teaching and Active Engagement).
- Display chart titled "Writers Decide!" (see Link).
- Refer to the "A Progression of Spelling Development" chart to see if students are ready to write sentences (see Conferring and Small-Group Work).
- Be ready to display an example of a "lift-the-flap book." We use *The Ultimate Book of Vehicles: From Around the World* by Anne-Sophie Baumann and Didier Balicevic (see Mid-Workshop Teaching).
- Gather colored paper and scissors for children to use to make flaps (see Mid-Workshop Teaching).
- Display and add to the "Writing Partners" anchor chart (see Share).

MINILESSON

CONNECTION

Share a brief story about making decisions about where to put things in a space. Explain that writers also make decisions.

"Writers, I have a quick story. Last Sunday, my little cousin and I made a castle out of blocks. We had to decide on a lot of things. We needed to decide how big the castle would be. We needed to decide on where the towers would be and how many we should have. We needed to decide on where the door would be. We wanted to make a bridge to the castle, but where should that go? There were lots of decisions to be made.

"The reason why I am telling you this is because writers get to make the same kind of decisions."

❖ **Name the teaching point.**

"Today I want to teach you that *every* time you start a new page, you get to think about how the new page will go. You are both the author and the illustrator. You decide everything—where the pictures will go, how big they will be, and what the words will look like."

TEACHING

Invite students to think with you as you study a page, talking aloud about the way the pictures and the words are laid out and then thinking about how you could try this in a book.

"Writers, I collected a few pages of books for us to look at together. Let's think together about how other authors and illustrators decided to put the words and the pictures on their pages."

I showed the class a page of a text that was filled with pictures and labels and began to think aloud. "Look at all of the things and pictures on this page!" I read some of the words. "This page has so many labels. Some of them are one word and some of them are two. Look at this big word here at the top!

"What do you notice about how the author and illustrator put the pictures and words on the page? Quick! Turn and tell the person next to you." I gave kids a moment to talk.

I called the group back together. "I heard lots of good observations. I heard you say that on this page, the author and illustrator put a lot of pictures, all over the page, with lots of labels. It's like this page is a 'whole bunch of stuff' about airplanes. These words here—*Air Travel*—are the heading of the page. The heading tells what the page is about.

"I bet the maker of this picture book thought about how she wanted the page to go, and thought, 'I want this page to show a whole bunch of stuff.'"

Return to the class book. Start a new page and demonstrate how you incorporate what you noticed from the mentor text.

I picked up our class book. "We could try what we noticed in our book about the classroom." I flipped to a fresh page in the class book. "The next page could be about the math center. Let's call this page 'math center.'" I wrote it big at the top of the page.

"What stuff could we put on this page?" Kids chimed in, and I quickly drew and labeled—the cubes, the pattern blocks, the counting bears, and the play money. Next to the money, I said and wrote "Clink, clink!" I said, "Neat, huh?"

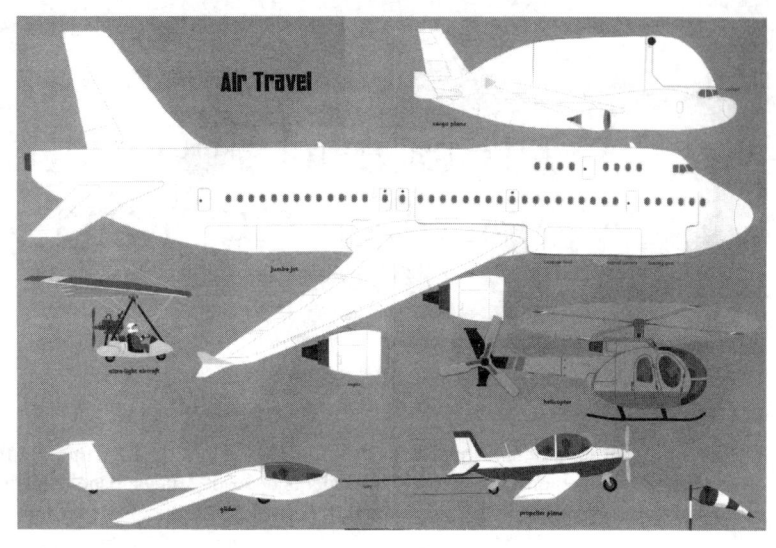

FIG. 8–1 From *The Ultimate Book of Vehicles: From Around the World* by Anne-Sophie Baumann and Didier Balicevic

You may not have heard these exact observations from your kids. Here, we invite students to think along with us, then shape their ideas to match our teaching point. The idea is not that kids guess the right answer, but that they are invited to think about author's purpose.

Choose any area in your classroom to write about that works for your class. It could be the sink area, the closets, the reading nook, anything that makes sense to you.

SHOW AND TELL WRITING: FROM LABELS TO PATTERN BOOKS

ACTIVE ENGAGEMENT

Invite students to try looking at a new page alongside a partner. Channel them to think about how the author decided to put the pictures and the words on the page.

"Writers, let's try this again." I shared another page. This time it was a page with one large drawing and sentences.

"Here's a different kind of page." I read the page. "What do you notice about the pictures and the words on this page? Is this a 'whole bunch of stuff page' or does it look a little different? Think about that for a minute." After providing a bit of thinking time, I invited students to turn and talk.

As expected, some students said things like, "There's a motorcycle" or "He's wearing a helmet." I called students back together and named what they were noticing in more transferable ways.

"I hear some of you thinking that this page is a little different. On this page, the author has one big picture and a few sentences to tell about it. What could we call this kind of a page?" Jason chimed in, "One big thing!" I continued, "Yes, let's call it that: a 'one-big-thing' page.

If your students have another idea for what it could be called, go with that. Also be ready to share out what you think it should be called. We don't expect every class to have a "Jason" who will call out exactly what you need.

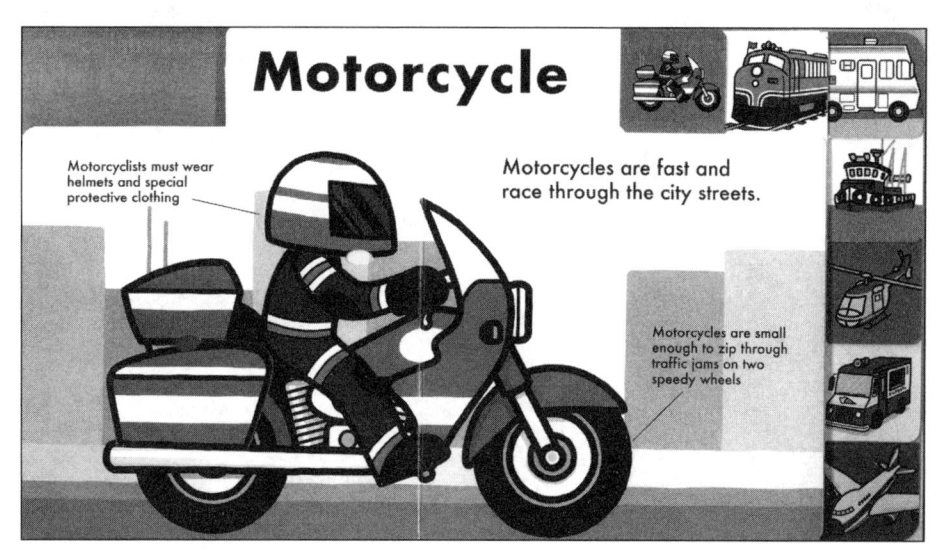

FIG. 8–2 From *On the Go* by Roger Priddy

"Interesting. I bet we could do that in our book about the school. Could we add a one-big-thing page? What would be so important that it should be really big on its own page?" A few kids chimed in with things like "the principal!" and "the yard!" and "the school bus!"

SESSION 8: WRITERS AND ILLUSTRATORS MAKE DECISIONS

"We could make a school bus, and our picture could fill up the whole page. Then, we could add sentences like 'This is the school bus. It is yellow. Kids ride on the bus.'"

LINK

Challenge writers to take risks and try new things in their writing. Remind them that there will be drawing time and there will be writing time again today.

"Writers, this is kind of neat, isn't it? Authors and illustrators like you make lots of choices and decisions about how to put their pictures and words on the page for their readers. Today, as you draw and write, you can ask yourself, 'How will I put the pictures and words on *this* page?' You might make a 'whole bunch of stuff' page or a one-big-thing page." I tacked up the "Writers Decide!" chart to the easel.

"This kind of decision making might be a little new for you. When we try new things, when we try tricky things, we can get that proud feeling. So today, when you try something new—like trying a new way for how a page could go—remember to feel proud!

"Today, we will start with drawing time, and then we will have writing time. Off you go!"

CONFERRING AND SMALL-GROUP WORK

Supporting Students Who Are Ready to Write Sentences Using Interactive Writing

TODAY'S MINILESSON OFFERED STUDENTS a vision of what their work could look like, and today you may want to refer to the "A Progression of Spelling Development" chart in the online resources to see if students are ready to write sentences. If they have filled up their pages with labels that have beginning and ending sounds, as well as two-word labels, they might be ready for sentences. You can convene a small group to get writers started with this.

In a small group, use interactive writing to help writers who are ready to write sentences.

Before you convene this small group, plan out a sentence you will construct through interactive writing with this group. Think about the high-frequency words and word parts that students need to work on. For the sentence in this sample, we chose high-frequency words, *here*, *is*, and *the*, because those are important words for students to know. To give all students access to this work, you'll probably want to plan on channeling different students to do different jobs during the small group. For example, one student might be in charge of writing the high-frequency words on each page, another student might be in charge of writing the first letter sounds, and another student might be the one who puts in the finger spaces.

Start your small group by saying, "Writers, you've grown—and so has your writing! Look at all the words you are writing. I think you are ready to graduate to writing sentences! Today I want to teach you that when you want to write a sentence, you say a word you want to write. If it is a snap word, just write it fast. If it isn't a snap word, then stretch it out and listen to the sounds."

You might suggest to the group that you want to write a sentence or a sentence strip to label your classroom door. "I want to write, 'Here is the door.' Could you help me write this sentence?" Then you'd want to plan out how the sentence would go, counting the number of words. Invite kids to help you by naming words that they know in a snap (*is*, *the*) and asking certain students to write the whole word on the sentence strip. While one student is writing the word on the sentence strip, engage the rest of the group in writing the word with their finger on their hand or with a marker on a whiteboard. You could also ask students to write the beginning and ending letters. Invite students to reread with you after each word is written and to help you leave spaces between words by placing a finger in between. After the interactive writing activity, invite kids to look at their own writing and think of what they'd like to put on the page.

MID-WORKSHOP TEACHING **Using Flaps to Make Books Fun to Read**

"Writers, I found another page that has something interesting that you could try." I showed the class a page of *The Ultimate Book of Vehicles: From Around the World* by Anne-Sophie Baumann and Didier Balicevic. "Look at this! Did you notice this book has flaps? When you lift up a flap, you see another picture and some words. That makes this page extra fun for the reader, doesn't it? Wouldn't it be neat to try this? We could call this a 'lift-the-flap' book."

"In just a moment, it will be writing time. So use the next few minutes to finish your drawings. During writing time, I will put some paper and scissors on your tables, in case you want to make flaps with words on your pages!" After about three minutes, I transitioned the class back to writing time.

As students are practicing in their own pieces, you can use prompts like:

- "Say it before you write it."
- "That's a word you know in a snap. Look at the snap word chart to help you."
- "Reread."
- "Remember to leave a little space. You can use your finger."
- "Stretch out the words and listen for the sounds."

To close the group, debrief the transferable work, saying something like, "You can do this all the time from now on. You can write another sentence on this page. Then you can do it on every page in your folder. Remember to say the words and write one word at a time, pausing to reread."

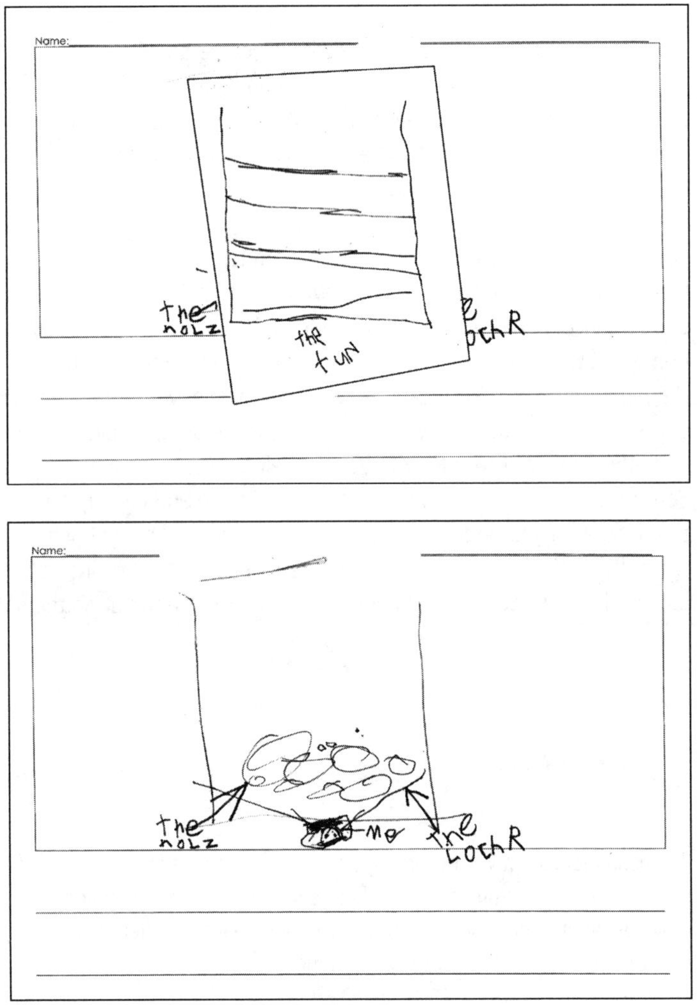

FIG. 8–3 Cora added a flap to her book about the park. The flap reads, "the tunnel." Under the flap reads, "the holes, me, the launcher."

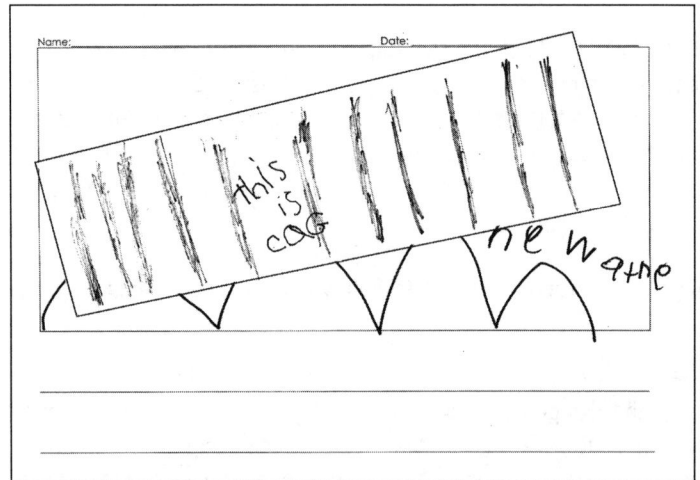

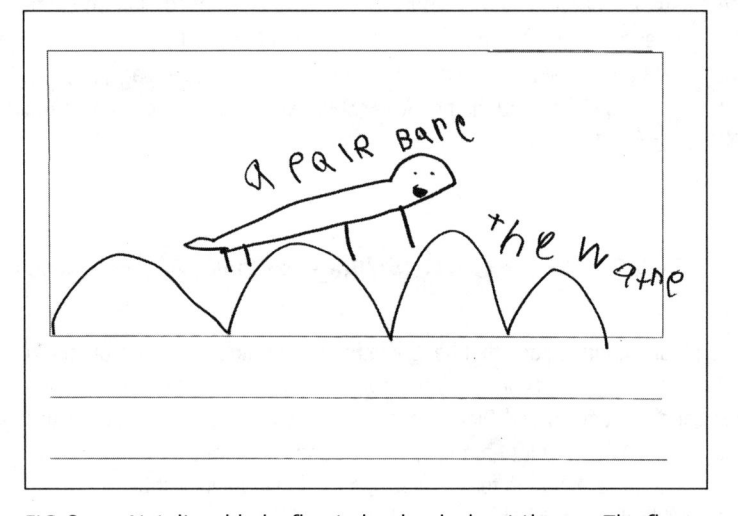

FIG. 8–4 Natalie added a flap to her book about the zoo. The flap reads, "this is a cage." Under the flap reads; "a polar bear, the water."

48   SHOW AND TELL WRITING: FROM LABELS TO PATTERN BOOKS

SHARE

Giving Compliments to Other Writers

Explain that writing partners often give compliments to help each other feel proud. Reveal a chart with some predictable language for compliments.

"Writers, you've been sharing your writing with one another and talking about your work. One thing that can help others feel proud is when you tell them something that was good that you noticed about their writing. It's called a compliment. Compliments help other people feel proud."

I added a Post-it titled "Give compliments" to the "Writing Partners" anchor chart. "When you give compliments to your partner or any writer, you can give a high-five or say, 'Good work!' You could tell them your favorite part and point to it. You could even notice something they worked really hard at."

ANCHOR CHART

Writing Partners

- Put one book in the middle.
- Read and talk.
- Ask questions.
- Add more.
- **Give compliments.**

"Partner 1, share a page of your book with your partner. Then, Partner 2, give a compliment! After you finish, Partner 2 can share their writing. Go ahead, partners!"

SESSION 8: WRITERS AND ILLUSTRATORS MAKE DECISIONS

49

Session 9

Adding Longer Labels to Bring Pages to Life

GETTING READY

- Before class, choose a page in your class book to use as a demonstration text. We use a page about the table and chairs (see Teaching).
- Be sure children have their writing folders (see Active Engagement).
- Display and add to the "To Write a Show-and-Tell Book" anchor chart (see Link). 👋
- You may want to refer to the "A Progression of Spelling Development" chart as you confer with children (see Conferring and Small-Group Work). 👋
- Find a piece of student writing that uses the high-frequency word *like*, or be ready to write a sentence using *like* on a whiteboard (see Share).
- Display the "How to Learn a Word" anchor chart from Kindergarten Unit 1, *Making Friends with Letters*, of the Units of Study in Phonics (see Share). 👋

IN THIS SESSION

TODAY YOU'LL teach students that writers put more details on their pages by adding more words. You'll work with children to study a page of a demonstration text to find places to bring the page to life with longer labels. Then you'll ask children to generate longer labels for their own writing.

TODAY YOUR STUDENTS will continue to draw and write books. Expect to see students labeling at least three things per page with some two- or three-word phrases.

MINILESSON

CONNECTION

Share a story about a cooking show where the chef was incredibly descriptive in her language. Rally students to use descriptive language to bring their pages to life.

"Writers, last night I watched a cooking show all about baking cakes. The chef, the person cooking, didn't just *show* the cake that she baked, she also *described* a lot about it. She said things like, 'This is a dark chocolate cake,' and 'It is soft and springy,' and 'It smells like melted chocolate.' I could practically smell and feel that cake, even though it was on my TV!

"It got me thinking. The chef *could* have said, 'Here's the cake.' But instead, she used words that helped me know even more.

"That got me thinking more. Maybe you could do the same thing with your show-and-tell books that the chef did with the cakes. You could make your readers feel like they're standing right in the store or the mall or the aquarium. Would you be game for trying to do that?"

SHOW AND TELL WRITING: FROM LABELS TO PATTERN BOOKS

🍀 **Name the teaching point.**

"Today I want to teach you that when writers want to show and tell as much as they can, they write longer labels (or even sentences) to bring their pages to life. It helps to write in ways that tell readers what things feel like, smell like, look like, sound like, or even taste like."

TEACHING

Invite children to help you study a page from your class book to find places to bring that page to life with longer labels. Then, write the labels on the page, voicing over ways you stretch out words and use the snap word chart.

"Let's continue working on our book about the classroom. We can add more information to each page so that our readers feel like they are right here in our classroom. Let's look at the part about the tables and chairs." I placed the demonstration text on the easel.

"Now, if we want to bring this page—and this place—to life, I think we need to add words that show what things feel like, look like, sound like, taste like. Let's try it."

I paused, looking at the picture, pointing to different parts. I pointed to the tables and said, "What do the tables look and feel like?" I looked over at the tables in the classroom as if studying them. "They're smooth and blue!" students shouted.

"There we go! The label could be 'the smooth table.'" I counted each word on my fingers as I said it. Then, role-playing a timid writer, I said, "*Smooth*, that word is hard, and 'The smooth table' is a lot of words. I don't know if I can do this. What do you think?" I asked the class.

The class shouted, "Be brave!" I nodded my head, took a deep breath, and wrote the words next to the drawing of the table.

"Let's try the same thing with the chairs. What do they look like? How do they feel? How do they sound?" Kids craned their heads to look at the tables. Some students said, "They're red and blue. They squeak." I said, "Yes! We could add in 'the squeaky chairs' right here next to the chairs." I wrote the words on the page.

Debrief in a way that's transferable.

"Wow! Now you could bring this book home and show your grandma and she would know that our tables are smooth and our chairs squeak! It would make her feel like she was right here in our classroom. We thought about what the things in our picture felt like, looked like, and sounded like. Then we wrote longer labels to show all those details."

Your goal here is to get kids to say more. Using their five senses is just one means to that end. There's no need to create graphic organizers or worksheets that force students to use their five senses for their writing. There are other ways to say more—by writing snap words or answering the questions "Who? What? Where? What?" and adding that to their words and picture.

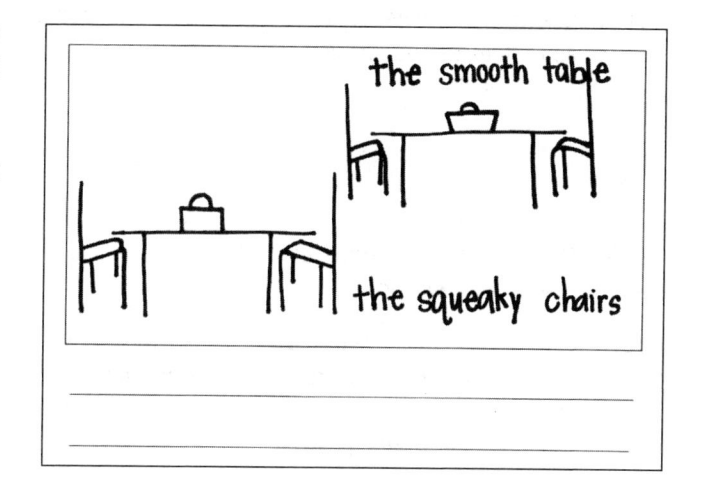

Here we choose to write the words conventionally. You might want to photocopy the class book and put it in kids' book bins for them to read during reading workshop time. Alternatively, you could choose to spell inventively to give students another opportunity to see an example of that.

ACTIVE ENGAGEMENT

Recruit children to look at their own writing to generate longer labels that will bring their pages to life. Coach in as students work, and then highlight a few phrases and sentences students suggested adding.

"Now you try it. Pull out a book from the 'done' side of your writing folder. Look around your picture. Think about what things feel like, look like, sound like, and taste like.

"Turn and tell your partner what words you can add to bring that page to life." I walked around listening in and trying to get kids to say more with prompts like, "What else does it look like? Touch another part of your drawing and tell what you could write there."

I called students back. "Writers, Marisol is going to add 'the soft grass' to her drawing of the yard. Patrick is adding 'this is sharp' above the drawing of a knife in his kitchen. His readers will know to be careful. Those words definitely help bring their pages to life!"

Notice we are sharing what we heard and not calling on students. We share out to provide clear examples of how students could do this work in their own writing.

LINK

Remind students to incorporate labels that bring their pages to life in their own writing today. Set students up for drawing and writing time.

"Guess what, writers? You have the power to make your reader feel like they are in your special place. When you write books, especially books where you're trying to show and tell as much as you can, you can bring your pages to life with longer labels. Today, we'll start with drawing time again. Draw all the details about what things look like, feel like, smell like! And then, when it's writing time, remember that you can bring your page to life with longer labels." I added the new Post-it to the "To Write a Show-and-Tell Book" anchor chart.

ANCHOR CHART

To Write a
Show-and-Tell Book

- Think of an idea.
- Tell all the parts.
- Draw and write the parts.
- **Write more! Bring pages to life.**

"Off you go!"

CONFERRING AND SMALL-GROUP WORK

Giving Students Extra Practice with High-Frequency Words

IN TODAY'S SESSION, your goal is to get students to write longer labels, elaborating and teaching even more. One way students can do this is by using high-frequency words to create phrases. Some high-frequency words are decodable (*me*, *am*, *at*, *it*), and other high-frequency words cannot be decoded (*the*, *of*). Either way, it is important for students to recognize these words quickly and write these words with automaticity—in a "snap." You'll want to be sure that students are set up to do this work—make sure they have access to a snap word chart (whether it is called that or not). Some students may require extra practice with certain high-frequency words. You might look to the extension sections from Unit 2 *Word Scientists: Using the Alphabet Chart to Start* of Units of Study in Phonics for kindergarten to help meet these students' needs.

As you are planning your high-frequency word instruction, use the high-frequency word lists from the assessment section of the second phonics unit to see which words your students know and which ones they need to work on. If you are not using our Units of Study in Phonics, we recommend introducing at least three high-frequency words a week to your class outside of writing workshop. In most classrooms that are using our phonics units, teachers tuck in small daily routines to help students learn high-frequency words. During transition times, you might play games, such as going on a word hunt or playing "I Spy." Many teachers also incorporate the high-frequency words into their morning message, leaving a word out and asking students to practice writing that word on the chart. You might also read an enlarged poem or a song with the words in it, then invite kids to identify and highlight high-frequency words.

In a small group, support kids in learning and using high-frequency words.

Prior to today's session, look at your assessment data to decide which students to focus on during a small group focusing on high-frequency words. We recommend choosing just one or two words to emphasize. Gather students in a small group with their writing folders and pencils. You may need whiteboards, depending on the warm-up you choose. Start your small group by doing one of the high-frequency word activities from *Word Scientists*. Then have students try to add those words into their writing.

Choose one of these word work activities as a warm-up:

- Go on a word hunt. Rally students to look all over the room, at all the charts, all of the print for the high-frequency words you are studying. You could even ask them to open up their writing folders and see if they could find it there.

- Act out a sports move while spelling the high-frequency word. For example, you might act out dribbling a basketball and say a letter every time you "bounce" the ball, then say the whole word as you "shoot" the ball. You could swing a tennis racket, throw a football, shoot a hockey puck, and so on. (See Units of Study in Phonics, Grade K, Unit 2, *Word Scientists*, Session 5, Extension 3.)

- Play "Snap Word 'Simon Says.'" Students will need a whiteboard and marker. You might say, "We're going to play 'Snap Word "Simon Says."'' Remember to do exactly as I say! Simon says write *the* in the middle of your board. Simon says erase it. Now write *the* really big on your whiteboard. Uh-oh, Simon didn't say!" Continue the game for several rounds. You might prompt students to: write snap words big, small, in the top corner, in the bottom corner; write a word twice;

MID-WORKSHOP TEACHING   Starting Your Words on the Left

"Writers, now that you're writing a lot of words on your page, you'll want to remember the thing that all writers know. We write our words from left to right."

I held up my page and pointed to where I planned on writing words. "Right now will you point to where you are going to start writing your words? Slide your finger to where you are going to keep writing words. Move from left to right!"

SESSION 9: ADDING LONGER LABELS TO BRING PAGES TO LIFE

write it all lowercase, all uppercase; and so on. (See *Word Scientists*, Session 10, Extension 2.)

- Sing the high-frequency word. Any two-letter word can be sung to "Twinkle, Twinkle, Little Star." Four-letter snap words can be sung to "Row, Row, Row Your Boat." (See *Word Scientists*, Session 13, Extension 2.)

Once you've warmed up by practicing the high-frequency word, challenge students to use the word to help them say more in their writing. "Now let's use this word to help us say more. Take out your writing. Point to your picture and try using the snap word to help you say more." You might need to model this work with your own drawing. Point to your picture and say, "The kids" or "Look at the kids," depending on the words you are emphasizing. Encourage children to try this work in their own pieces, in more than one place. They may try adding to their labels or adding a sentence to their page.

Close your small group by reminding students that they can learn any snap word by doing the activity you did; they could do it at home or on the playground. Then tell them *why* it's important. "These snap words can help us say even more in our writing. They can make it even easier for our readers to read our writing and know exactly what we mean!"

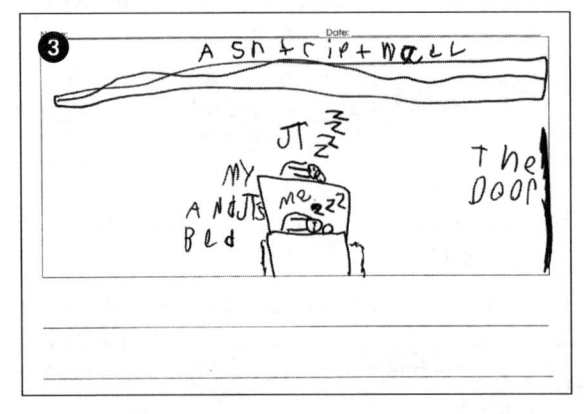

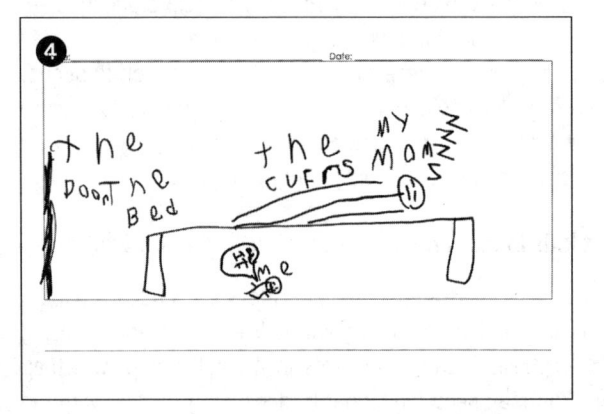

FIG. 9–1 Andrew's book about his house. He went back and added high-frequency words. (*Page 1:* I like my house. *Page 2:* my things, the X box, the start of the hallway, me, the shelf, the ottoman. This is the downstairs. *Page 3:* A striped hallway, my and JTs bed, me, the door. *Page 4:* the door, the bed, the covers, my mom, me.)

SHARE

Turning Words into Snap Words—*Like*

Highlight a piece of student writing to teach a high-frequency word and review the process of learning new words.

"Writers, put your writing on the 'still working' or 'done' side of your folder and come to the rug. I have to share with you what Julio told me about his grandma. He's writing a show-and-tell book all about her. I asked him to say more, and he said, 'My grandma smells like perfume. She smells good!' Doesn't that help us know more about his grandma? If she were here, she'd smell good! *Like* is a special word. I bet a lot of you could use this word in your books."

I wrote "My grandma smells like perfume" on the whiteboard. I underlined *like*. "The word *like* is important enough for us to work hard to learn it, the same way we've learned *the* and *me* and *my* and all the other words on our snap word chart.

"Let's do all the things that we know to learn a word in a snap." I brought out the "How to Learn a Word" anchor chart from the Units of Study in Phonics, Kindergarten Unit 1, *Making Friends with Letters*, and I coached students through the steps to learn the word *like*. While studying the word, kids noticed that it ended in the letter *E*, but they couldn't hear that letter when they said the word.

Once they'd learned the word, I said, "Could you use this word in your own writing? You know it now for whenever you need it!"

No need to worry if you cannot find a piece of student writing with the word like. *Instead, you could write a sentence or phrase about the school cafeteria using the words* smells like. *Your main goal in this share is to teach children a high-frequency word that they will need as they move forward, especially in Bend III.*

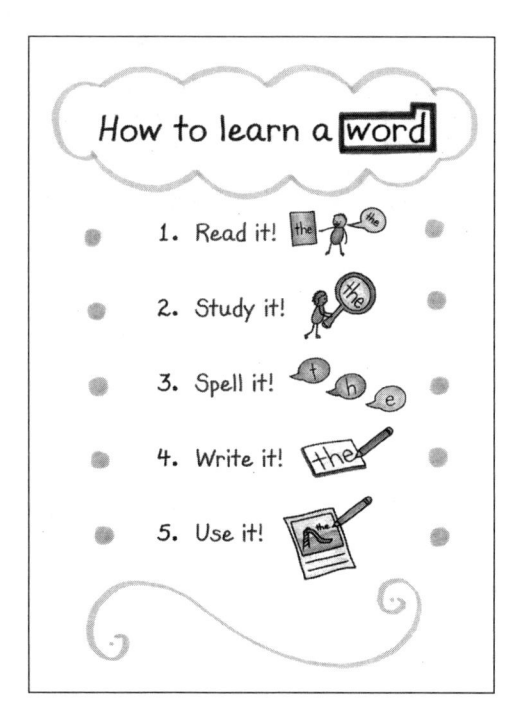

How to learn a word

1. Read it!
2. Study it!
3. Spell it!
4. Write it!
5. Use it!

SESSION 9: ADDING LONGER LABELS TO BRING PAGES TO LIFE

Session 10

Writing Sentences that Say What Pictures and Labels Can't

GETTING READY

- Be ready to add a sentence to a page of the class book as your demonstration text. We use a page about the library (see Teaching).
- Display and add to the "To Write a Show-and-Tell Book" anchor chart (see Link and Share).
- Ensure you are providing just-right paper choices for your students (see Conferring and Small-Group Work).
- You may want to refer to the "A Progression of Spelling Development" chart as you confer with children (see Conferring and Small-Group Work).
- To prepare for the next session, ask a fifth-grade teacher (or a teacher in another grade) if her students could visit to talk to your students about their writing. See Session 11 for more details.

IN THIS SESSION

TODAY YOU'LL teach students that writers can touch their page and say a sentence that tells what the whole page is about. Then they try their best to write that sentence, one word at a time. You'll demonstrate how you think about a sentence and then write that sentence, using all you know about spelling.

TODAY YOUR STUDENTS will continue to draw and write books. Expect to see some students writing sentences in their books, using tools such as the snap word chart, the alphabet chart, and the "Brave Spellers" anchor chart.

MINILESSON

CONNECTION

Invite students to see how they can use sentences to say where things are or what things are for.

"Writers, yesterday during writing time, I was working with Jerome on his book about his bedroom. I pointed to his picture and asked, 'What's that?' Here's how the rest of our conversation went."

> **Jerome:** Oh, that's my dresser. It has my clothes in it.
>
> **Teacher:** You should write that.
>
> **Jerome:** Where? I don't have any room in my picture for all those words!
>
> **Teacher:** Well, maybe you could write a *sentence*.

"I bet a lot of you are just like Jerome and there are things in your pictures that you could say more about."

✤ Name the teaching point.

"Today I want to teach you that you can write sentences to tell readers about what's on your page, like where things are or what things do. The words you know in a snap can help you."

TEACHING

Demonstrate how you touch your picture and generate sentences to teach even more.

I held up the class book about the school. "Help me do this with our book about our classroom. Let's touch a page and say something more about it, like what something is or what it does." I held up the page about the library.

I touched the page and said, "Library." I paused for a moment. "Wait, that's a label. I can push myself to say more." I asked myself, "What does it do?" I pointed to the page and said, "Oh! This is the library. We read here. Yeah, those are sentences that tell what this is *and* what it does. That certainly teaches more!"

Take students through the step-by-step process of writing a sentence.

"Now we're ready to write the sentence, 'This is the library.'" I touched the page as I said the words. "Let's say the first word, *this*. That's a snap word, so we can use the snap word chart." I looked over at the snap word chart, then wrote *this* on the page. I repeated this for the next two words, saying them, checking the snap word chart, and writing them. When I got to the last word, *library*, I said, "*Library*, that's not a snap word. We have to stretch that one out." I slid my right hand down my left arm and said the word slowly. Once students had said the word a few times, I wrote the letters while looking at the alphabet chart. Then we read the sentence together, as I pointed under each word.

    This is the library.

Debrief in a way that is transferable.

"We can point to our picture, think about what something is or what it does, and say a sentence about that thing. Then we can be such brave spellers and do our best to write every word, one by one."

ACTIVE ENGAGEMENT

Invite students to write the next sentence with you.

"Do you think you could help me with the next sentence? We can write 'We read here.'"

    We read here.

We are choosing to write the word library *conventionally so you can photocopy this class book and put it in kids' book bins. You could choose to stretch out the word* library *and write it using inventive spelling.*

SESSION 10: WRITING SENTENCES THAT SAY WHAT PICTURES AND LABELS CAN'T   **57**

"Let's say the first word—a snap word. We can write that quickly. Everyone, your finger is a magic pen. Write the word *we* on your hand."

While the class wrote the word *we* on their hands, I called a student up to write the word on the page of our book. I continued in that fashion. A student wrote the first letter in *read*. I wrote the rest of the word. Another student wrote the word *here*. As she was writing, she looked at the snap word wall.

Once we finished writing the sentence, I said, "Now let's read our sentence and check it. Did we get every word? Yeah! Way to go, brave writers!"

LINK

Remind writers that from now on they can write sentences on their pages using the snap word chart and the alphabet chart.

"I'm going to add, 'Write more! Write sentences!' to our chart. This will remind us to write sentences that teach our reader even more about what things are and what they do.

"I bet you are going to be writing a lot of words today! Will you point to a tool in the room that can help you in case you get stuck?" Kids pointed to the snap word chart, the alphabet chart, and the "Brave Spellers" anchor chart.

Be sure to have the "Brave Spellers" anchor chart displayed prominently in your classroom and remind kids to refer to it often as they write.

ANCHOR CHART

To Write a
Show-and-Tell Book

- Think of an idea.
- Tell all the parts.
- Draw and write the parts.
- Write more! Bring pages to life.
- **Write more! Write sentences.**

Write more!
Write sentences.

CONFERRING AND SMALL-GROUP WORK

Predictable, Quick Interventions to Keep the Whole Class Writing Lots!

DURING TODAY'S WRITING TIME, you'll want to move quickly among your students, channeling them to work with energy and independence.

Match children to paper choice that provides just-right goals for volume.

Look to your writing center to evaluate the paper choices you are providing students. You will probably need to add some choices that have two, three, or four lines on a page. The number of lines on each page should be based on your expectations for each writer. You'll want the page itself to act as a sort of challenge for the writer, as if the page is calling "fill me up."

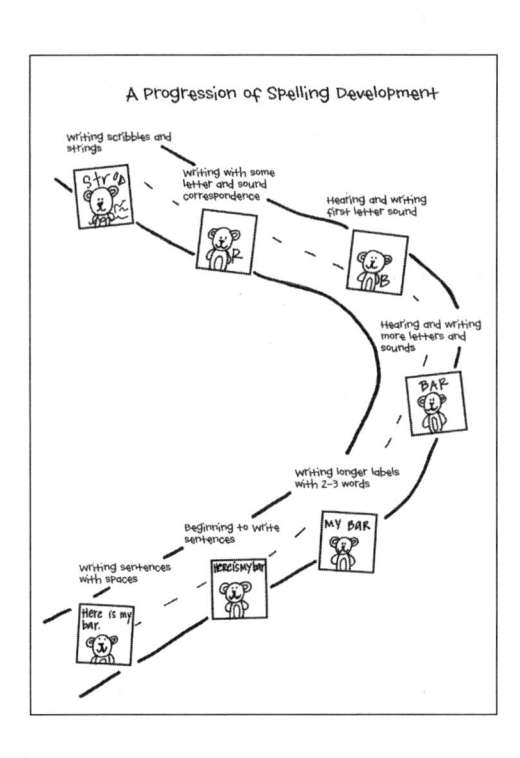

Expect that some students won't be ready to write sentences yet.

You might find that a few students are not yet ready to add sentences to their pages. You'll want to be sure your expectations match students' zone of proximal development. Take note of what students are doing with independence and try getting them to go to the next level, not three levels above that. Look to the "A Progression of Spelling Development" chart to assess where students are and what their next steps might be. If they are writing salient sounds, see if they can isolate and write the beginning sounds. If they are isolating beginning sounds, see if they can start to hear ending sounds. If they are hearing beginnings and endings, see if they could try for medial sounds or add high-frequency words to their labels.

Keep an eye out for writing process.

Make sure students are moving through the writing process, adding to their drawings and their words, then starting new pieces. Rally them to try to add sentences to each of their pages. Keep in mind you might have some students who have just become ready to try to add labels, and they are working on trying to add more and more labels. Once they have added to the pictures and words at their level, encourage them to get started on new piece. Remind them to touch and tell, sketch across the pages, then write their words.

MID-WORKSHOP TEACHING   **Remind Students to Remember to Reread, Especially When Writing Lots of Words**

"Writers, now that you are writing lots of words, you might notice that sometimes when you are writing, you forget what you want to say! Sometimes you even skip a word. So here's a trick. It helps to reread your page often. Point to each word as you read it. Then you'll remember what comes next."

SESSION 10: WRITING SENTENCES THAT SAY WHAT PICTURES AND LABELS CAN'T

SHARE

Taking Stock and Making Plans

Invite children to show their books to partners and assess how much they have written—how many words, sentences, pages.

"Writers, bring a book to the meeting area." When students had gathered, I said, "Will you show your partner how much you wrote? Count the number of words you wrote today!"

After the children counted, I said "Who wrote sentences today? Who wrote more than one page?" Thumbs went up, and I signaled that yes, this is the sort of volume I expected. "If you didn't write that much today, push yourself tomorrow. You can't teach a lot if you don't write a lot."

Channel students to reread their writing and say what they'll do to make their writing even better tomorrow.

"Let's reread what we wrote and think about what we could do tomorrow to make our writing even better. Let's use our chart 'To Write a Show-and-Tell Book' to help you talk to your partner about how you can make your writing better for tomorrow."

After a minute, I said "Turn and tell your partner what you're thinking. You might say 'Tomorrow I'm going to . . .'"

I needed to support some partnerships by pointing to and rereading the chart. I voiced over to students, "I hear Sonia saying that she's going to work on bringing her pages to life.

"Tomorrow will be a special writing workshop. Some fifth-graders will be coming to talk with us about our writing! I can't wait for them to see all you have been doing!"

Session 11

Growing Writers Talk about Their Writing in Important Ways

IN THIS SESSION

TODAY YOU'LL teach students that writers talk about their writing by sharing what they are making, what they are proud of, and what is tricky. You'll demonstrate how writers do this, role-playing both teacher and writer.

TODAY YOUR STUDENTS will continue drafting and revising their books, while talking to and conferring with fifth-grade students about their writing. At the end of the session, they will celebrate their writing with a gallery walk.

GETTING READY

- ✓ A day or two before this session, you'll want to ask a fifth-grade teacher (or a teacher in another grade) if three or four of her students could visit to talk to your students about their writing. They should arrive at your classroom during the link (see Link, Conferring and Small-Group Work, Mid-Workshop Teaching, and Share).
- ✓ Display the "Writers Talk about Their Writing" chart (see Teaching).
- ✓ Be sure children have their writing folders or a piece of writing with them during the minilesson (see Active Engagement).
- ✓ You may want to give copies of the "Compliment Conference Tips" sheet to fifth-graders (see Conferring and Small-Group Work).
- ✓ Download, prepare, and hand out labels or cards that say *brave speller*, *detailed drawing*, and *favorite part* to students to put on parts of their books (see Share).

MINILESSON

CONNECTION

Announce to students that they will be talking about their writing to some special guest visitors.

"Writers, I was at a party last night and one of the people I talked to is a writer. Just like you! That writer talked to me about what's going well with her writing and what's not going so well. I even gave her some ideas about how to make her writing better! That conversation made me think about you. You talk to me about your writing. And you talk to your classmates about your writing, too. I bet some of you go home and tell your families about your writing projects. And that's what writers do. They talk about their writing because it is important.

"Guess what! Today, I invited some special visitors—fifth-graders—to talk with you about your writing! And they are coming in just a few minutes!"

❖ **Name the teaching point.**

"Today I want to teach you that writers talk about their writing. When writers talk about their writing, they can talk about what they are making, what they are proud of, and even what is tricky."

TEACHING

Demonstrate ways that you can talk about your writing. Play the role of both the writer and the teacher, using two chairs to shift between the two.

"Let's have fun with this. I'll pretend to be a kid *and* a teacher, as they talk about writing in a conference. I want you to watch the way that I talk about my writing when I'm a kid, because you'll get to do that with your partner in a minute."

I put my glasses on my nose. "Okay, so here I am as a teacher. I'm talking to the kid now."

 Teacher: Hi there! I see you are writing. How's it going? Tell me about your writing.

I scooted over to the other chair, took my glasses off, and held a piece of writing. "Now I'm the kid, answering the teacher."

 Student: It's going good! I am making a book to tell about the cafeteria. I am so proud of this page. It's my favorite.

I changed seats and shifted back to the role of teacher, then the student, and back to the teacher:

 Teacher: Wow! Look at the way you put so many words on that page. I bet you are proud. Is there anything that has been tricky?

 Student: Yeah, I don't know what to do next.

 Teacher: I can help with that!

Debrief, naming the ways writers can talk about writing and why it can be helpful.

"Writers, did you see how I talked about my writing as a kid? I made a little chart to help you remember these ways." I placed the "Writers Talk about Their Writing" chart on the easel, referring to it as I continued. "I said what I was working on, what I was proud of, and I even said what was tricky. The neat thing is, if you tell what's tricky, you can often get help!"

If getting students from a fifth-grade class or another grade to come into the room feels too tricky, you might instead coach students to talk with their writing partners. If you do this, you'll want to change the references so that students talk with a partner instead of a student from another grade.

"How's it going?" is a classic phrase borrowed from Carl Anderson. We love this phrase because it is conversational instead of confrontational. It sets students up to have a dialogue about their writing rather than setting them up to right away be taught how to do something.

We want students to be able to use this kind of growth mind-set language when talking about their work throughout their day. You could bring a lesson like this into reading, math, science, and social studies.

---

62   SHOW AND TELL WRITING: FROM LABELS TO PATTERN BOOKS

ACTIVE ENGAGEMENT

Assign partners to work in roles and use the "Writers Talk about Their Writing" chart talk in the same way. One partner will ask "How's it going?" and the other partner will talk about their writing.

"Writers, now it's your turn. Partner 2, you get to be the teacher and listener first. You get to say, 'How's it going? Tell me about your writing.' Partner 1, you get to talk about your writing. Remember that you can say what you are making, what you are proud of, and even what's tricky. Before we start, think for a minute about your writing and what you might say." After a moment or two, I continued, "Go ahead! Talk about your writing. Partner 2, help your partner use the chart to say more." After a minute or so, I invited students to switch roles.

LINK

Remind students that they can talk this way all the time about their writing.

"Wow, I think you grew as authors just now. I listened to you, and you sounded so sophisticated as you talked about your writing. So any time that you're chatting about your writing—with a teacher, with your grandma, with a classmate, or with a fifth-grader, you can talk about it in this way!"

Announce that the fifth-grade visitors who will be conferring with writers today have just arrived.

"I see the fifth-graders at our door right now! How exciting! Head to your writing spot and get set up. In a minute, I'll send a fifth-grader over to you. You'll get to talk to three or four big kids as you write today, and they'll help you start new books and finish your books. After that, we'll do some celebrating with just us. Off you go!"

CONFERRING AND SMALL-GROUP WORK

Compliment Writers on Their Growth

YOUR ROOM WILL BE BUZZING with conversations between fifth-graders and kindergartners sharing their writing. To ensure that your students gain lots of practice talking to others about their writing, you'll want to encourage the fifth-graders to rotate three or four times to new students, almost as if they were conferring the way you would during a workshop.

As you support the fifth-graders with giving feedback to your students, you might take this opportunity to reflect on how *you* talk to writers about their writing. According to Sheila Heen in *Thanks for the Feedback*, any time we talk to each other we are giving feedback. She says that usually our feedback falls into three categories: coaching ("try this," "keep this going"), appreciation ("wow," "I see you're trying," "amazing"), and

| **Compliment Conference Tips** ||
Look for . . .	You could say . . .
Habits and Routines	
Kids getting started writing without reminders	"You are the kind of writer who gets started all on your own!"
Kids keeping going: drawing and writing words	"Wow, you are like the little engine that could. You just keep going with drawing *and* writing!"
Kids finishing one book and getting started on another book	"Not all kids remember what to do next. You are able to be the boss of your writing. You must be proud!"
Writing Words	
Kids trying to write words—even long and tricky ones	"Look at you! You thought about the exact word you want to write and now you are bravely trying to get that down!"
Kids trying out their own spellings of words—even if they aren't "book spelling"	"Do you remember that in the beginning of this unit, you didn't write any words? Now look at you! You are writing one word after another!" "I can't wait to see how many words you're going to write! I'll shout you out to everyone and tell them how brave you are going to be!" "Show me some of the words you tried . . . What did you do to help yourself? . . . You can do that all the time!"
Drawing	
Kids making pictures with lots of details	"You didn't just draw . . . You also drew . . . And you drew . . . Wow! As the reader, I can learn so much from your picture." "This picture had so much information in it. You drew one part and then another and then another. Now your reader will know *so much*."

MID-WORKSHOP TEACHING **Giving Compliments about Pictures, Words, or Being the Boss of Their Own Writing**

"Writers, will you stop what you're doing right now?" I waited for writers to stop talking to the fifth-graders.

"Fifth-graders, this is for you. Look at your kindergartners' work. You are going to give them a specific compliment. It might be about their pictures, their words, or that they are the boss of their writing and got started on a new piece all by themselves. This is how a specific compliment could sound:

"You are the kind of writer who . . . "

"I'm noticing that you . . . "

"I admire the way you . . . "

"Fifth-graders, give your kindergartners a compliment! Kindergartners, after you receive a compliment, say 'Thank you!'

"Now, fifth-graders, find a new kindergarten author so they can talk with you about your writing."

evaluation ("you're doing this nicely"). If you're like most teachers, you might be giving a lot of coaching and evaluation, and maybe not a lot of appreciation.

Take time today to notice the growth students have made because of you. For some kids, that progress might be that they've gone from not knowing letters to writing words. For others, that growth might be that now they can stay in your room and work for the entire writing workshop, or talk to a partner about their writing. Celebrate these victories, and give yourself some appreciation for the progress your students have made. Then, pass those compliments on to your kids.

Compliment conferences that build agency and growth mind-set.

Today, you'll invite fifth-graders to confer with children and ask them about their writing. You might even give them the "Compliment Conference Tips" sheet to help them give compliments.

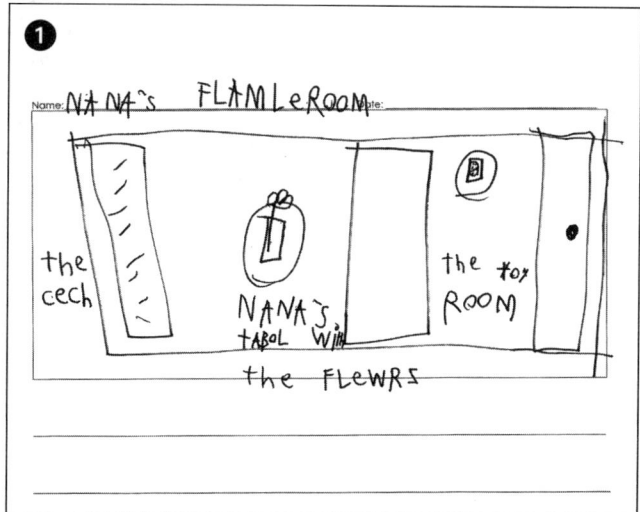

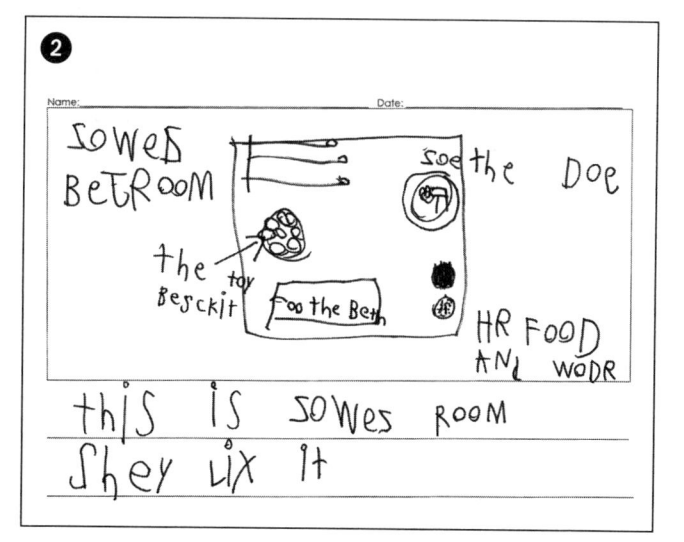

FIG. 11–1 Anna's writing about her grandmother's house. (*Cover:* My Nana House. *Page 1:* Family room, the couch, Nana's table with the flowers, the toy room. *Page 2:* Zoe's bedroom, the toy basket, the bath, Zoe the dog, her food and water. This is Zoe's room. She likes it.)

SESSION 11: GROWING WRITERS TALK ABOUT THEIR WRITING IN IMPORTANT WAYS

SHARE

Showing Off Our Books and the Proud Parts

Channel writers to mark the parts of their books that they are proud of. Then, engage the class in a gallery walk so that they can admire each other's work.

"Kindergartners, now it is time to celebrate you and show off your work to each other today. Fifth-graders, you can help. I've got a few labels for you to use—like stickers. They say *brave speller* and *detailed drawing* and *favorite part*. Soon, we'll walk around our room and you'll get to show off your books to your classmates and our visitors. But before you do that, will you work with a fifth-grade visitor to choose your favorite piece, and will you use these labels to mark up the parts of your writing? You can put them on the parts where you tried to be a brave speller or the part you made your best drawing, and your favorite part. Then, the world will know the parts you are especially proud of!"

Brave Speller	Detailed Drawing	Favorite Part

I gave students a minute or two to mark up their books. Then I invited them to walk around and look at each other's work as I played some classical music.

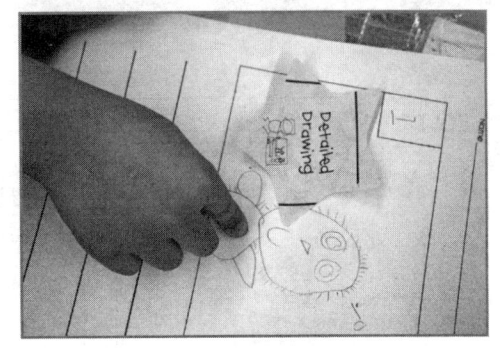

SHOW AND TELL WRITING: FROM LABELS TO PATTERN BOOKS

Using Patterns to Write Show-and-Tell Books

BEND III

Session 12

Writing Books that Kids Want to Read

GETTING READY

- Display "To Write a Show-and-Tell Book" anchor chart (see Teaching and Active Engagement).
- Be ready to write a book with the class in a booklet. You may want to clip it on an easel, so kids can see it as you write (see Teaching and Active Engagement).
- Put blank booklets on children's tables before they begin to write (see Link).
- Make sure each child has a book he or she wrote to share with a partner (see Share).

IN THIS SESSION

TODAY YOU'LL teach writers that they can write books that they wish existed in the world—about the people, places, and things that matter to them. You'll channel the class to write a class book together about a topic that's important to kids.

TODAY YOUR STUDENTS will write books about topics that matter to them across pages. Expect to see students writing one or two books today.

MINILESSON

CONNECTION

Rally students around the purpose of this bend—kids want to read books that matter to them. Suggest that they turn the classroom into a book factory, with children writing books they want to read.

"Writers, when you went home yesterday, I studied our library closely. I took all the books off the shelves and laid them on the rug. Guess what I noticed? Even though our library is filled with amazing books about airplanes and elephants and skateboards, it's missing a really important type of book—books about all of you and the things you love!

"This has happened in other classrooms, too. Did you know there are some classrooms where kids live near farms, and there aren't any books about farms! And in some classrooms, kids live with their grandmas, but there aren't any books about kids who live with grandparents! And in some classrooms, kids love robots, but there's not one book about a robot! This is a problem because it's important that books show and tell the people, places, and things that are important to the kids in the classroom.

SHOW AND TELL WRITING: FROM LABELS TO PATTERN BOOKS

"This all got me thinking. You've been showing and telling about the places and things that are important to you and you've gotten so brave at writing words on your page. You *are* authors and illustrators. Are you up for the challenge of writing books that show and tell the things that are so important to you?

"Great! Let's turn our classroom into a book factory! Factories make a *lot* of something—a lot of peanut butter, a lot of pencils, a lot of soccer balls. Our book factory can make a lot of books that show and tell the things that are most important to you. Once you've written a lot of books, we can make our classroom into a bookstore and share all of the great books you have written. We can even add your books to our library!

"What do you think?" Kids nodded. "I think this will be an important challenge."

❖ **Name the teaching point.**

"Today I want to teach you that writers write the books they want to see in their library, about the topics that are important to them. To do this, you can think, 'What are the people, places, and things that I wish there were more books about?' Then you can choose one and write a book about it, page by page, using all you already know."

Representation within children's books matters. Kids need books that act as both mirrors and windows. They need to see themselves and the things they care about, in addition to people who look different from them and have different experiences.

TEACHING AND ACTIVE ENGAGEMENT

Invite partners to brainstorm topics for books that kids want to read. Select a topic your students love and propose that the class write a book about that topic.

"You already know that to write a show-and-tell book, you first need to think of an idea." I tapped the first bullet on our "To Write a Show-and-Tell Book" anchor chart. "Here's what will be different: the thing you'll need to think about is, 'What are the people, places, and things that are important to me? What do I wish there were more books about?' Do you have some ideas? Turn and talk."

I voiced over ideas I heard and added on a few as students chatted. "Families! Apartment buildings! Monsters! Babies! Playing! Kids who are adopted!

"If our classroom becomes a book factory, you'll need to write *lots* of books. So let's write the first one together. Let's plan a book together about . . . birthdays. Do you agree that's a topic that's important to you? Do you wish there were more books about birthdays? Great!"

Guide students to help you plan, draw, and write a pattern book, using what they already learned about writing show-and-tell books.

"We've got an idea for our book. Now we have to think about how the parts will go." I held up a blank booklet and clipped it on the easel. "We could probably write about different things you see at birthdays on each page. What things do you see at birthdays?" Students called out, "cake, candles, balloons."

If students don't readily come up with ideas, fill in things you know are important to them.

SESSION 12: WRITING BOOKS THAT KIDS WANT TO READ

"Next, we have to write the parts. Let's write a pattern book. What could it sound like? Maybe it could go, 'Look at the . . . '" I paused.

"Cake!" several kids chimed in.

"There you go. Turn and tell your partner what could go on the other pages of this book about birthdays. Say the parts across your fingers and use the words 'Look at the . . . ' to help you talk like the book."

After a minute, I called them back together. "So here's one way our book could go," I said as I got ready to touch the first page. "Look at the cake." I turned and touched the next page. "Look at the candles." I turned the page once more. "Look at the balloons.

"What a book! And what a cool topic!" I looked to the chart again. "Let's start to draw and write the parts." I wrote "Birthdays" on the cover. Then, I quickly sketched a picture of a cake on the first page of the book and added the line, "Look at the cake."

We suggest that you finish this book today, either in front of kids at another point in the day or on the side without them. You can make copies of the finished book and give it to kids to add to their book baggies and read during reading workshop.

LINK

Rally students to write a whole book about a topic that matters to them today. Call on a few children to share their topics before sending the whole group off to write, using all they know to help them.

"Writers, our library needs books that show and tell about *you* and the things that are important to you. Do you think you can write a *whole* book today, using all you already know? What will you write about today in a book for kids? How will your book sound? When you have an idea, put a thumb up." I called on a few kids to share their ideas before sending the whole group off.

"I'm going to write about my favorite noodles 'cause my daddy makes the best noodles. It will go, 'This is ravioli. This is macaroni. This is spaghetti,'" said Adira.

"I'll write about what I do at after school. I like to read. I like to eat snacks. I like to play chess," said Emily.

"So many ideas! I've placed new booklets for you at your tables, so you can get started right away! Off you go!"

In this unit, pattern book writing is a scaffold to support students' transition to sentence writing. If students need more support writing sentences, you might scaffold the child's sentence writing by saying, "I bet that book could sound like . . . " and then suggesting a possible pattern back to them.

CONFERRING AND SMALL-GROUP WORK

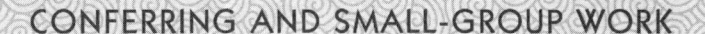

Supporting Volume Right from the Start of a New Bend

AS YOU DID AT THE START of Bends I and II, you'll want to use your conferring and small-group work time today to move from table to table and from child to child, getting the work of this bend up and running. You will rally your children around the call to write books that kids want to read, books about the people, places, and things that matter deeply to them. At this time in their writing development, your kindergartners will benefit from repeated practice and writing lots of books, so you will want to encourage your students to write at least one whole book today. You'll also want to encourage kids to write sentences across the pages of their books, not just labels.

Use these voiceovers to support student practice.

To support a quick transition from the minilesson to writing:

- "Don't forget to write your name and stamp or write the date. This writing is yours!"
- "Take our your tools like the alphabet chart and your snap word collection. Use them to help you."
- "Our library can't wait for your books! Look how many of you have already gotten started!"

To promote generating ideas:

- "Think about things kids like you like to do. Then write that book!"
- "Think about the books you want to read! Then write them!"
- "Think about things that are important to you. You can be the one to write those books."

To promote planning across pages:

- "Touch and say what will go on the first page, the next, and the next."
- "What sentence could you write on that page?"
- "Draw your pictures across the pages, and then write your words on each page."

To promote volume and stamina:

- "Writers don't just write one book! Try to write two today!"
- "Don't get stuck on tricky words. Spell them the best you can! Be brave and move on!"
- "Reread what you have so far, then ask, 'What will I write next?' Then write it!"

MID-WORKSHOP TEACHING
Do Your Best and Then Say "Next" at Tricky Words

"Writers, let me give you a tip. If you want to write *lots* of books in our book factory, that means you'll have to write the whole time. If you are writing, and you get to a tricky word like *monkey* or *basketball* or *playground*, you'll need to spell the word the best you can, and then say, 'Next!' and keep going to the next word and the next page. Don't let tricky words stop you and slow you down. Spell them the best you can and then say, 'Next!'"

SHARE

Trading and Reading Books

Explain that today, kids will read each other's books, just like during reading time. Channel students to introduce their books, sit back to back, and read.

"Writers, come quickly to the meeting area. Today, you wrote books that are about things that are important to you, books you think should be in our library. Other kids will be dying to read these books!

"So let's have some reading time! You'll read just like during reading workshop. The only thing that will be different is that instead of reading books from your baggie, you'll read the book written by your partner. First, you'll introduce your book to your partner. You could say something like, 'This is my book. It's about . . . Enjoy!' Then, start reading, back to back on the rug."

I helped students exchange books and get started reading back to back. As they read, I voiced over, "Read the pages of your partner's book. Look at the pictures and point to the words."

After a minute, I called the class back. "How cool was that! You read books written by your classmates. Give your partner a high-five and say, 'Thanks for the book!' as you trade it back."

Session 13

Talking and Writing with Patterns and Snap Words

IN THIS SESSION

TODAY YOU'LL teach writers they can write pattern books using high-frequency words. You'll demonstrate by using the high-frequency word chart to think about how a book could go.

TODAY YOUR STUDENTS will continue to start and finish writing books about topics that matter to them across pages. Expect to see students writing books with patterns, using the high-frequency chart to help them spell.

GETTING READY

- ✓ Be ready to display the chart, "Snap Words You May Know (including More Snap Words"). Write the high-frequency words from the chart on Post-its and put them over the words on the chart. Display this chart near your easel and use it throughout this session (see Connection).

- ✓ You may want to refer to "A Progression of Spelling" chart from Session 10 (see Conferring and Small-Group Work).

- ✓ You may want children to refer to their own collection of snap words as they write, if you are doing phonics or word study instruction, alongside or prior to this unit (see Conferring and Small-Group Work).

MINILESSON

CONNECTION

Share a story about finding a bunch of high-frequency words in the classroom. Reveal a chart with these words and set partners up to read the words.

"Writers, gather close. You're not going to believe this, but something funny happened last night. I was moving some of the books in our library around, so there would be space for all the new books you're writing. And guess what happened? Some of the words fell out of the books! I picked them up, and I was about to put them back, when I thought—'Wait! We could use these words in our book factory!'"

I revealed a chart with a large number of familiar high-frequency words. "You know these words in a snap! Read over them with your partner."

Snap Words You May Know (including More Snap Words)			
Snap Words You May Know			
a	an	and	at
here	I	in	is
it	like	look	me
my	see	the	this
More Snap Words			
are	can	to	

These high-frequency words have been taught in the Units of Study in Phonics. If you are not teaching from our phonics series, it will be important to teach these high-frequency words. Be sure to include the high-frequency words that your students know well so they can use those words to write simple pattern books.

❖ **Name the teaching point.**

"Today I want to teach you that when you want to write a book with a bunch of pages, sometimes it helps to talk and write in a pattern. You can use the words you know in a snap to write sentences in a pattern book."

TEACHING

Demonstrate how you use the high-frequency words from the chart to help you brainstorm different ways your book could go.

"Watch how I use these words to help me. In a minute, you'll get to try it, too. First, I need an idea. Hmm, . . . what's another book I could write about something important and interesting, a book that belongs in our library . . . maybe . . . dancing? You're always showing me your dance moves. Our library definitely needs a book about dancing!

"Now, I need to use the words I know in a snap to make sentences. How could this book sound?" I pointed around the chart of words. "Hmm, . . . well, it could say, 'I like spinning. I like jumping. I like twisting.'" As I said the high-frequency words I moved the word Post-its off the chart and stuck them to the whiteboard to show how they could help make a

Here, you highlight two possible sentence patterns to emphasize that there are many different ways that books can sound and go. Within this bend, ensure that students are flexibly using the snap words they know to write different patterns across books.

SHOW AND TELL WRITING: FROM LABELS TO PATTERN BOOKS

sentence. "But that's not the only way it could go. It could also say, 'Look at me spin. Look at me jump. Look at me twist.'" Again, I moved the snap words to help make a sentence.

"Tell your partner how else this book could go." I listened in as kids talked, reminding them to use the snap words to help them. "Wow! There are so many ways this book could go. Now I can choose one and write this book."

ACTIVE ENGAGEMENT

Invite partnerships to share the topics for their next books. Choose one student's idea and ask partners to brainstorm possible patterns for that book using the words on the chart.

"Thumbs up if you have an idea for your next book. Turn and tell your idea to your partner. Say, 'My book will be about . . .'" I listened in to grab an idea all students would know about to practice with.

"Sienna wants to write a book about pets. We definitely need more books about pets in our library! She thought it would probably have pages to show and tell about all her special animals: a dog, a cat, a fish. But how could the words go? Hmm, . . . turn and tell your partner one way the book could sound. Use the words on the easel to help you."

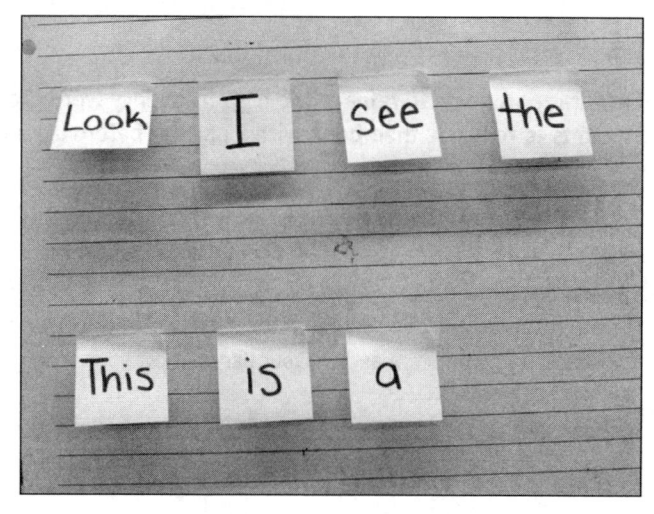

FIG. 13–1 Teacher making sentences out of high-frequency words.

I harvested a few patterns to share out. "Sienna, listen to some of these patterns and tell us which one you might use. 'This is a cat. This is a dog. This is a fish.' Or, 'Look at my cat. Look at my dog. Look at my fish.'" Sienna shared the pattern she liked most.

Choose another student's idea and offer repeated practice in generating a pattern. Again, ask students to brainstorm possible patterns using words on the chart.

"I heard Anna say she wants her next book to be about snacks that the kids in this class love, like apples and crackers and raisins. How could her book sound? Quick! Use the chart to help you.

"Lots of ideas here!" I shared some of the patterns, then asked, "Anna, what pattern do you want to use?" She said, "We like."

As you listen in, you may hear some students construct sentences that don't quite sound right. If a child says, "Look cats," you'll want to accept their approximation and then say their sentence back to them, lifting the level of language. You might say, "Yes, you could write, 'Look at the cats!' That would be a great book for you to write."

You may want to make an adjustment here if you notice the lesson seems to be going long. If that is the case, you can remove this second opportunity for practice from the active engagement.

SESSION 13: TALKING AND WRITING WITH PATTERNS AND SNAP WORDS

LINK

Encourage students to refer to the high-frequency word chart to help them as they write their books. Invite students to rehearse their book with a partner before leaving the meeting area.

"Writers, remember that when you want to write longer books, it can help to write in a pattern. You can use the words you know super well, in a snap, to help you write patterns. Using those words will make your books even easier for other kids to read.

"Think about the book you'll write today. How will each page go? What words will you use again and again? Before you head off to write, turn and tell your partner how your book will go."

FIG. 13–2 Paula's pattern book about fashion. (*Cover:* Fashion. *Page 1:* Look at the skirt. *Page 2:* Look at the sunglasses. *Page 3:* Look at the boots.

CONFERRING AND SMALL-GROUP WORK

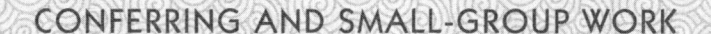

Supporting Students across a Range of Writing Development Stages

BEING A KINDERGARTEN TEACHER is a tricky business. You'll likely have students who are at widely varying stages of writing development. Some students may have just transitioned from writing strings of letters to hearing and recording salient sounds, and are not yet ready to write sentences. Some students will be writing multi-word labels, and you'll be coaching them to write sentences. Other students will be writing sentences across pages more independently, choosing the high-frequency words they need and using them to generate and write patterns.

Support Students Who Are Working to Hear More Sounds in Words

Students who have recently transitioned from writing strings of letters to hearing and recording salient sounds will need to continue to fill up their pages with labels, working to hear more and more sounds in each word they write. Resist the temptation to make fill-in-the-blank pattern books for students who aren't ready to do this work on their own. Instead, you may want to refer to the "A Progression of Spelling Development" chart in Session 10 for help in making the decision about what the next step might be for particular students.

Use Oral Rehearsal to Help Students Plan Pattern Books across Pages

You'll probably find students who need support planning how a pattern will go across their book. We recommend you ask students to orally rehearse their pages, so you can pinpoint what students are doing well and where they could use additional support. After asking a child what he or she is writing about, you might say, "What will you write on every page?" If a child tells you the content of each page, perhaps saying, "This page will have the hoop, and the next is going to have the ball, and the next is going to have the court," you might follow up by celebrating what the writer is doing well and suggesting a next step. "Wow! It sounds like your book will show all kinds of basketball things. What a good plan! Have you thought about how your book will sound? Tell me the words you'll write on the pages."

If the child still needs support, you might direct her to her collection of high-frequency words, if you are doing phonics and word study instruction alongside or prior to this unit. "Look at the words you know in a snap. Can you make those words into a sentence that could go in your book?" If a child still has difficulty, you might help her generate a pattern. "What is the pattern that starts, 'I . . . '?" or "Maybe it could say, 'Look at the ball' or 'I see the hoop.'"

You may find it helpful to say back the writer's plan before you leave. "You are writing a book about basketball that kids will *love!* On every page, you'll show something about basketball." Continue as you touch each page. "You said your book will go,

---

MID-WORKSHOP TEACHING
Writing Snap Words, Fast and Furious

"Writers, eyes on me so I can give you a tip. The nice thing about having words on the snap word chart is that you can use them to help you spell. But I'm seeing some of you looking at a word and saying one letter, then writing one letter, then looking again, and then writing again." I looked up and down, up and down, dramatizing how long that kind of process takes.

"Doing that takes a long time, and it doesn't help you learn the word. When you want to a learn a word, it helps to look at the whole word and all the letters and then try to write all of them down, fast and furious. Then you can look up again to check your word. Watch me." I quickly demonstrated looking at the word *the*, writing the whole word, and then checking it.

"So from now on, when you write your snap words, look at the word, and then write the whole thing fast and furious before you check it!"

SESSION 13: TALKING AND WRITING WITH PATTERNS AND SNAP WORDS

'Look at the hoop. Look at the basketball. Look at the court.' I can't wait to admire this book!" With this kind of conference, you'll have set your student up to write a whole book. Expect to have many conferences like this across the bend.

Encourage Flexibility in Writing: Writing with Patterns and without Them

Although your minilesson emphasized writing a pattern book, that doesn't mean that all students need to write pattern books. In fact, the pattern is a scaffold to help students plan and get words down on the page. Some kids might write books that look more like the all-about books they'll write later in the year, with a bit of information on each page. For instance, a child might write across a three-page booklet, "My dog loves to eat food. I like to play with dogs. Dogs are really fun." If you see kids who are writing books that tell a bit of information on each page *without* a pattern, encourage them to do this again and again across a variety of topics. Not all books need patterns.

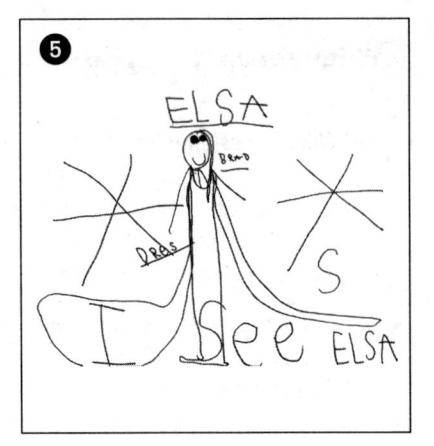

FIG. 13–3   Lucia's pattern book about the movie *Frozen*

78

SHOW AND TELL WRITING: FROM LABELS TO PATTERN BOOKS

SHARE

Imagining How Books Could Sound

Invite students to compose ways a shared class book could go using snap words. Emphasize the importance of making your sentences sound like the sentences in books.

"Writers, these words helped you write more and more today." I gestured toward the snap word chart. "Tell your partner some of the sentences you wrote." I moved among the partnerships, celebrating what kids wrote.

"Can I give you one tip that will help you make your sentences even stronger? Here it is. When you write sentences in books, you want your sentence to sound just like sentences sound in books. Let's try this together. Let's imagine we want to write a book about the playground. That's a great topic for kids, right?"

I placed the words *see look the* together on the whiteboard. "See . . . look . . . the . . . slide. Wait! Does that sound right? Does that sound like a sentence in a book about the playground?" Kids shook their heads.

"Let me try again and you can help me make it sound right. What if I start with the word *see?* What word would sound right next?" Kids chimed in with words like *my* and *the*. "Oh, maybe *the* would work." I placed *see the* on the whiteboard. "See the . . . slide. Does that sound like a book? Yes! We could say, 'See the slide. See the swings.' How could the next page about the playground sound?" I gave students a moment to talk.

Then I coached students to try a few more possibilities, including some that sounded like a book and some that didn't. After each attempt, I asked students to evaluate whether the sentence sounded like a book and to revise it if it didn't.

- "Here the slide."
- "Look at the slide."
- "This a slide."
- "I like the slide."

Session 14

Studying How Sentences Look

GETTING READY

- Write two simple sentences from a book on sentence strips. (Hang this sentence up for reference in your classroom. It will be used again in Session 18.) (see Teaching).

- Be ready to interactively write a new sentence with students in the class book (see Active Engagement).

- You may want to gather a few different kinds of pattern books to show during small-group work—a lift-the-flap book, a question-and-answer book, a knock-knock joke book, or a see-saw pattern book (see Conferring and Small-Group Work).

- Have a blank booklet ready to demonstrate writing a book without a pattern (see Conferring and Small-Group Work).

- Provide flaps and extra paper (see Conferring and Small-Group Work).

- Display or create the "Special Announcement" sign for students to edit (see Share).

IN THIS SESSION

TODAY YOU'LL guide students to study the conventions of a sentence. You will help students notice that sentences start with an uppercase letter, contain mostly lowercase letters, have words separated by spaces, and end with a punctuation mark.

TODAY YOUR STUDENTS will be starting new books and going back to books they have already started, using the word wall to form patterned sentences. Those students who are ready will pay special attention to capitalization and punctuation.

MINILESSON

CONNECTION

Gather writers together and ask them to name the topics of their next books.

"Book factory writers, gather quickly! I have something important to teach you that will help you write lots of books that other kids can read. Let's not waste a minute. Our bookstore will be opening in a few days.

"Last night, I was thinking about our book factory and the important books you are making. I was so excited I couldn't sleep. Will you think about the next book you will write that belongs in our library? When you have an idea, put your thumb up. If I point to you, will you name what your next book will be about, loud and proud?"

I pointed to five kids who shared ideas. "Fairies!" "Toys!" "Computers!" "Monster trucks!" "Games!"

"What important topics! These books will help you show and tell other people so much about you. Let me give you a tip that will help you make sure other kids can read your books."

❖ **Name the teaching point.**

"Today I want to teach you that when writers like you write sentences in books, there are things they always do. They work to make their sentences look like the sentences in a book so that they are super easy for readers to read."

TEACHING

Show an example of a sentence from a book and invite students to notice its features. Mark up the sentence as you talk about the important conventions. Then, share another example and channel students to notice how it has similar features.

"Let's study a sentence from a book to see what writers always do. Here's a sentence from *The Zoo*. I'll read it, and will you see what you notice about this sentence?" I revealed the sentence I'd written on a sentence strip and pointed under each word as I read it.

Here is the zoo.

"Do you notice anything about how this sentence looks? About how it starts and ends? Turn and talk." I listened in for a moment, curious to see what students noticed on their own.

"Let's look at how this sentence starts. It has an uppercase letter." I marked up the sentence as I spoke. "Let's see how it ends. It ends with this little mark. It's called a period. It helps us know this is a telling sentence. Lots of you said there were spaces between the words. Here, here, and here. And do you see how most of the words have lowercase letters? When you write your sentences, you can try to do these things too."

"Let's check another sentence from the book and see if this next sentence has the same parts." I revealed another sentence strip. "Wow! This sentence has so many of the same parts. What do you notice about this sentence? Tell your partner."

ACTIVE ENGAGEMENT

Engage the class in an interactive writing of a sentence, sharing the pen to highlight the uppercase letter in the first word, spaces, and punctuation at the end.

"Let's write a sentence right now, together. And as we write, let's try to do all the things that writers do when they write sentences.

"How about we write a page for the book about dancing? It could say, 'Look at me spin.' Let's say it together before we write it." We said the sentence a few times.

For this session, you may substitute any book from your leveled library that has a simple pattern and simple sentences. You will want to choose a book with short sentences without internal punctuation or special capitalization.

"Keep in mind how sentences look as we write this sentence. *Look*. That's the first word in the sentence. What kind of letter do we need at the beginning? That's right, an uppercase letter. Write it in the air. Check the alphabet chart if you need to." I called one student up to write the uppercase *L* and then I finished writing the rest of the letters in the word.

I continued to write the sentence interactively with students. I invited a student to come up and use their finger to help us keep the spaces between words.

Several times, I shared the pen with students and invited all students to write-in-the-air as one student added to the class book, saying:

- "Everyone, write the word *at* in the air. Remember to use lowercase letters. Use the snap word and alphabet chart to help."

- "Let's end this sentence with that little dot, a period. This sentence tells something, so it can end with a period."

I pointed under each word and we reread the sentence. "Wow, writers! This looks like a sentence in a book. When we do all the things writers do as they write, it makes our writing *so* easy to read."

LINK

Channel writers to try to make the sentences they write look like the sentences in books.

"Writers, you've got a lot to do today. Most of you will head off and start on a new book, one that will help you show and tell all about you. Make sure it's a book that tells something important about you and the people, places, and things you care about. Write the books you think should go in our library!

"As you write in our book factory today, work hard to make the sentences you write look like the sentences in a book. Remind your partner what you should do when you write sentences." I gave children a half a minute to brainstorm. "I can't wait to see you try this new learning as you write your books today! Off you go!"

If students still need support forming the letter, be ready to voice over the letter formation pathway or the way to make an uppercase letter L. You might say, "Line down, little line out." Write the letter in the air, following that pathway as you say the words.

During interactive writing, a student may make a mistake while he or she is writing in the class book. Use this to create a quick, teachable moment. If a child writes ta *for the word* at, *you might say, "Let's look carefully at the word* at *on the snap word chart. What did Alex get right here? What do we need to change?" Then coach him through making the changes, so that he crosses out the word and writes it correctly.*

CONFERRING AND SMALL-GROUP WORK

Writing Different Kinds of Pattern Books, Books without Patterns, and Fancy Beginnings to Books

Y OU MAY HAVE STUDENTS in your classroom who have been writing sentences since the beginning of the year. To support and challenge them, you might lead small groups, inviting them to try writing more complicated patterns or a book without patterns. You might also teach them how to generate fancy leads for their books, and then channel them to generate multiple possible ways their books could begin.

Invite students to try another kind of pattern book.

- Bring a few kinds of pattern books to the group, maybe a lift-the-flap book, a question-and-answer book, a knock-knock joke book, and a book with a see-saw pattern.

- Name why you gathered the group together. "Writers, you have been writing so many pattern books! I thought you could change up the pattern books you've been writing by studying how other authors organize their patterns. Will you study these books with me to see how these authors write their patterns?"

- Pass out pattern books and help students notice and name what the authors did. They might notice that the author wrote a riddle on the flap like "What's brown, small, furry, and lives in the ground?" Underneath it says, "A mouse." You could say to students, "It seems like the author wrote a riddle on the flap and the answer underneath."

- Help students plan out how their book could go. "Will you think right now about what kind of pattern book you want to make? Will it be a question-and-answer book? Or a knock-knock joke book? Once you know what kind of book it will be, think about how it might go. Here's a fresh new booklet. Will you touch and tell how your book will go?"

Show students how to write an all-about book *without* patterns.

- Name why you gathered the group together. "Writers, you've written a ton of pattern books! I think you're ready to write a book that *doesn't* have a pattern! A book where you teach everything you know about a topic."

- Briefly demonstrate how you write a book without a pattern. "Will you help me plan out how my book could go? First I could write, 'Spaghetti is my favorite food.' Hmm, . . . what could I write next? Maybe I could write, 'It has red sauce and long noodles.' How could my book end? Maybe, 'I like it when there are meatballs on top.'" I touched and turned each page in the book as I said each sentence.

- Channel students to orally rehearse how their books will go. "Think of something you want to teach all about . . . a place you go, a thing you love. Now think about everything you know about that thing. Touch and tell those things across the pages! Go!"

MID-WORKSHOP TEACHING   **Showing Off the Places Where You Made Your Sentences Look Like a Sentence in a Book**

"Writers, will you find a place where you tried to make your sentence look like a sentence in a book? Put your finger on that sentence. Did you write an uppercase letter at the start of the first word? Did you add periods at the end of your sentences? Did you leave spaces between words? If you're missing something, add it in or change it now.

"Great, turn and show off your sentences to the person next to you."

After a minute, I said, "Back to writing. This time, make sure that each sentence you write looks the way sentences look in our books!"

SESSION 14: STUDYING HOW SENTENCES LOOK

83

- Transition students to writing and coach in as they write. "Get started writing that book! Use the snap word chart to help you write words you know in a snap, and be brave when you get to long, tricky words. I'll coach you as you work."

Challenge students to make a fancy beginning for their books.

- Name why you gathered the group together. "Writers, how your books begin is so important. One thing you are ready to try is to make the beginnings of your books even better."

- Channel writers to study mentor texts to notice how they begin. "Let's look at these books and think about how they started." You might show a book that starts with a question and another book that starts with a big idea. "What did they do to hook their reader? Turn and tell your partner." Help students name what the author did.

- Coach students as they write beginnings for their books. "Take out a book you've already written. Say a few new, different beginnings. Which one do you like best? Write it!" After students have fixed up the beginning for one book, encourage them to try making fancy beginnings for all their books. You might have to provide flaps or more paper, so they can add their extra sentences.

FIG. 14–1 Robbie went back to his pattern book about iPads and added a first sentence—his opinion about iPads.

84   SHOW AND TELL WRITING: FROM LABELS TO PATTERN BOOKS

SHARE

Interactive Editing

Invite the class to make choices about uppercase and lowercase letters and punctuation, as you engage in an interactive editing session.

"Writers, put your writing away and come to the rug. You worked hard to write your sentences today. Earlier, you noticed that words in sentences mostly have lowercase letters. The first word in the sentence starts with an uppercase or capital letter. Your names start with capital letters, too.

"I was thinking we should start getting ready for our bookstore in a few days. Last night, I asked my little cousin to help me make a special announcement sign to let people know about it. Before we post it, let's make sure that it looks just right." I clipped the writing to the easel and read the announcement to the class.

"Hmmm, . . . it looks like there are four things that need to be fixed up in this letter. See if you can find them with your partner."

After giving students a minute to turn and talk, I invited students to help me fix up the letter. "Many of you noticed that this letter *W* in *we* should be uppercase or capital. As José fixes it, turn and tell your partner why it needs to be that way."

Each time we fixed up a part of the letter, I encouraged students to tell their partner why the letter needed to be changed.

FIG. 14–2 *Top:* Announcement with mistakes written in. *Bottom:* Announcement fixed up by students.

SESSION 14: STUDYING HOW SENTENCES LOOK

85

Session 15

Slowing Down to Leave Spaces between Words

GETTING READY

- Write a sentence with no spaces, "hereisthebook," on a sentence strip or chart paper. Be ready to cut apart the words and put them on an easel (see Connection).
- Be ready to demonstrate writing sentences with spaces in your class book (see Teaching).
- Provide whiteboards and dry erase markers to students (see Active Engagement).
- Make available the snap word chart and alphabet chart for kids to refer to as they write. Be ready to write new words on Post-its, if needed (see Conferring and Small-Group Work).
- Display the "Writing Partners" anchor chart (see Share).

IN THIS SESSION

TODAY YOU'LL teach writers that they can make their writing easy to read by slowing down to leave spaces between words. You'll demonstrate how you use your finger as a tool to help you leave spaces between words.

TODAY YOUR STUDENTS will continue to write books about the things that matter to them. Expect to see them writing books with at least a sentence on each page, approximating spaces between words.

MINILESSON

CONNECTION

Show a note that you received that was hard to read because of the lack of spaces between words. Then, cut the words apart to show that spaces make a sentence easier to read.

"Writers, last night I got a note in my mailbox on top of this book. It looks like this." I revealed a sheet of paper that read:

    Hereisthebook.

"I've been looking and looking at it, and I just cannot figure out what it says! I see some letters I know inside, but it's so hard to read. There are no spaces between the words! Let me cut it apart and make some spaces." I cut out each word and spaced them out on the easel. "Wait a minute! Can we read this? Do you see some words you know? Let's point and read."

    Here   is   the   book.

"That makes sense! Much better, right? This note was so hard to read when it was all smushed together. And kindergartners . . . sometimes, your writing looks like this smushed-up note."

SHOW AND TELL WRITING: FROM LABELS TO PATTERN BOOKS

❖ **Name the teaching point.**

"Today I want to teach you that when writers write books that others will read, they help make their words easy to read by leaving spaces between their words."

TEACHING

Demonstrate writing a sentence, emphasizing how you use your finger as a tool to help you leave spaces between words.

"Let me show you what I mean. Let's keep going on our book about dancing. The next page could read":

Look at me jump.

"As I write, I want you to watch what I do to help me leave spaces. I always point and read. And I use my finger to help me leave a just-right-size space. Spaces aren't hard to do, but they are easy to forget if you go too fast!"

Before writing, I said the sentence again as I pointed to where the words would go on the page.

Look . . . at . . . me . . . jump.

I continued to write, word by word, leaving spaces as I went and placing my index finger down before writing the next word. I put a period at the end of the sentence.

"Can you read the words? Point and reread with me." We read the sentence together while I pointed under each word.

"Do you see how I wrote one word and then used my finger to help me remember to leave a space before I wrote the next word? Now my words aren't smushed together and we can point to each one!"

ACTIVE ENGAGEMENT

Pass out whiteboards and challenge students to write a sentence with spaces between words. Select a sentence for the whole class to try.

"Your turn to try!" I quickly passed out whiteboards. "Another page in this book could read":

Look at me twist.

"Let's say it together before we write it." We repeated the sentence as a class.

Children at this age are still building their sense of word vs. sentence. Taking words and separating them is a good way to help children understand what words are and how they compose a sentence.

Since our teaching point is about finger spaces, we aren't spending a lot of time on stretching out each word. You will have time to help kids stretch words out during conferring and small group.

SESSION 15: SLOWING DOWN TO LEAVE SPACES BETWEEN WORDS

"Do your best to write this sentence. Use your finger to help you leave spaces between each word." I moved around the meeting area to coach students. As students approximated, I voiced over:

- "Use the words on the chart here to help you write the snap words."
- "Reread as you go!"
- "Use your finger to leave a space."
- "Check to see that you are leaving spaces!"

Before I brought the class back together, I said, "Check your sentence next to the sentence we studied yesterday. Does your sentence look like the sentences in books? It should have an uppercase letter at the beginning, spaces between words, and punctuation at the end."

I asked students to erase their boards.

LINK

Challenge writers to write in ways that are easy to read. Support writers in naming the topic of their next book.

"Writers, today, will you be the kind of writers who write sentences that look like the sentences in books? You can use the words on the snap word chart to help you spell *and* you can use spaces between your words to make your sentences easier to read by leaving spaces. Use your finger to help you leave a space, or who knows, maybe you'll invent another way to help you remember to leave spaces.

"Before you leave the rug, will you tell your partner what your next book might be about? You might need to finish a book from your folder, but after that, you'll want to start a new one right away." After children planned for a moment, I sent them off.

The goal of getting students to practice this is to support them as they are writing snap words, leaving finger spaces, and adding in punctuation. You're not expecting kids to know how to write the word twist *accurately. You might have students in your class for whom any of this work feels very hard. Let them do their best to get as many letters down as they can.*

CONFERRING AND SMALL-GROUP WORK

Predictable, Quick Interventions to Keep the Whole Class Writing

SOMETIMES, WHEN YOU INTRODUCE NEW CONVENTIONS like the ones in the last two sessions, it can slow the pace of kids' writing to a crawl. To help remedy this, you'll want to give lots of reminders to keep up writing stamina and give compliments that support students' approximations. You can invite writers to do the best they can, get their writing down on the page, and then perhaps reread and fix it up. Coaching students in conferences and small groups to use all they know will help your writers remember the bigger work of the unit, too.

Coach children in conferences and small groups to use what you've taught them.

Idea generation and planning:

- "Think of something you love or that other kids love. Maybe it's a place, or something kids do, or something kids like."
- "Touch and tell how the pages of your book will go. Then draw your pictures."

Oral rehearsal:

- "Say the whole book before you write it. How will it sound? Now, write that book."
- "Before you write the sentence on the line, say it a few times. Write that whole page."

Rereading while writing:

- "Before you write the next word, read what you already have. Then, write the next word."
- "Reread! What word will you write next?"

High-frequency words:

- "You can spell that word in a snap. Look at the chart and try that word again."
- "That word isn't on the chart, but you can make it a snap word. Let me put it on a Post-it for you."
- "Look at the word and study it. Then write the whole word and check it."

Inventive spelling in sentences and labels:

- "Do your best to be brave and spell that word. Say it slowly. What sounds do you hear? Write down the letters."
- "Try that word again. Let's say it slowly together to see if you hear even more sounds."
- "Make sure you are using the alphabet chart to help you."
- "Spell it the best you can and keep going."

MID-WORKSHOP TEACHING

Suggesting Ways to Remember to Leave Spaces

"Writers, look at you write! You are working hard to leave spaces between your words. This is making your books so much easier to read. Some of you are using your finger to help you. I've seen some of you flip your pencil over and use it to help you leave a little space." I demonstrated doing this. "Or, you could imagine that you need to leave a space the size of your pinky toe or a tiny pebble or a teeny piece of popcorn. As you keep writing, do whatever you need to do to help you remember to make a just-right-size space. Back to your writing!"

SHARE

Writing Partners Compliment Each Other on Their Sentences

Encourage partners to read each other's writing and give compliments.

"Writers, bring a favorite book that you've written to the carpet and sit next to your partner. Will you take some time to share your writing with your partner?" I gestured to the "Writing Partners" chart. "This time as you are working with your partner, will you touch each word as you read it?"

After a couple of minutes, I said, "Writers, will you give your partner some compliments on how they made their writing easier to read?" I pointed to the "Give compliments" Post-it. "Notice and point to it if they used a capital letter. Tell them if they used a period or exclamation point. Give them a high five if they left spaces between words." I paused to let kids compliment each other for a minute.

"Nice! I see lots of high-fives!"

SHOW AND TELL WRITING: FROM LABELS TO PATTERN BOOKS

Session 16

Writers Write More Sentences on a Page

IN THIS SESSION

TODAY YOU'LL teach writers that they can write more than one sentence on a page by rereading and thinking about what else they can say. You'll demonstrate rereading the class book and using the snap word chart to help you add another sentence.

TODAY YOUR STUDENTS will continue to write books about topics that matter. You might see them writing two sentences on each page. Some students will go back to previously finished books to add more sentences to each page.

GETTING READY

- Be ready to demonstrate how to add a second sentence to a page of writing that already has one sentence in your class book (see Teaching).
- Make available the "Snap Words You May Know (including More Snap Words)" chart from Session 13. Be sure you have word Post-its on each word on the chart so you can use them to make new sentences. Also be sure kids have access to the "My Vowel Chart" and the alphabet chart (see Teaching and Conferring and Small-Group Work).
- Have a second page of your class book ready with one sentence for kids to add to (see Active Engagement).
- Before class, prepare copies of booklets that contain just pictures—perhaps one book shows dogs and another shows snacks. You may want to use images from online sources, in books, or on stickers. Hand out booklets to each partnership (see Conferring and Small-Group Work).
- Before class, prepare baggies or pouches with high-frequency words from Session 13. If you are teaching from the Units of Study in Phonics, your children can use their high-frequency word baggies from the second Kindergarten unit, *Word Scientists: Using the Alphabet Chart to Start* (see Conferring and Small-Group Work).
- Make available revision strips and tape in a basket in the writing center (see Mid-Workshop Teaching).
- If you or your students are not familiar with the tune to "Happy" by Pharrell Williams, you may want the class to listen to the song ahead of time. There's a link to the song in the online resources (see Share).
- Display lyrics to "The Writing Song!" (see Share).

MINILESSON

CONNECTION

Reiterate the importance of writing books that matter.

"Writers, the work you are doing writing books is so important. You have ideas for books that matter to you and matter to other kids. Your writing absolutely matters to this classroom and the world. In a few days, we're going to open our bookstore, and everyone will get to read all these amazing books you've made!

"Yesterday, after you left, I reread our book about dancing, and I realized, we probably have more to say in this book! I have lots of things I know about dancing. How many of you think you have more to say about your topics: could you say more about mermaids and trucks and dogs?"

❖ **Name the teaching point.**

"Today I want to teach you that you needn't stop writing after just one sentence. You can write as many sentences as you want on a page. To write more, it helps to reread a page and ask, 'What else could I say?' Then you can write that sentence down, using all you know."

TEACHING

Emphasize how instead of moving on, writers think about what else to write and then write it. Demonstrate rereading and adding another sentence to the page by using snap words and stretching out words they may not know.

"Will you help me try this? I want to add another sentence to the book about dancing. First, I need to reread what I already wrote. Here's the first page: 'Look at me spin.' I bet I can write more. Hmm, . . . what else can I say on this page? Whisper to your partner what you think I might write."

I gestured dramatically toward the chart, "Snap Words You May Know." "I bet I could use these words to help me add another sentence to my writing. Maybe I could say . . . " I reached for the word Post-its on the chart and took the words *I* and *can* and placed them on the whiteboard. I stretched the words *spin* and *fast* out quickly to make this sentence, "I can spin fast." I said, "That's one sentence I could add.

"What other sentences could I make? Maybe I could write, 'It is fun!' or 'I like spinning' so my readers know how much I like it." As I talked, I formed each sentence out of snap word Post-its and stretched out words like *fun* and *spinning* that were not on the chart, and then I wrote each sentence in the book.

"Do you see how I thought about 'What else I could say?,' then took these snap words from the chart to help me think of three more sentences I could add to my book? Did you also see how I wrote the snap words quickly and then stretched out the other words? I could write all those sentences on my page."

To help your students come up with more ideas for what they could add, you might remind kids to ask the question "Where?" or "What?" You could also have them think about how things look, what they smell like, taste like, or sound like to help them add to their writing.

Showing kids how you manipulate the snap words to make different sentences is a powerful visual for kids. It reflects the work they are doing during phonics.

ACTIVE ENGAGEMENT

Reread the next page of the class text. Invite students to think with a partner about what other sentences they could write on the page. Quickly revise the page to include a new sentence.

"Your turn to try it. Let's read the next page together. Point in the air as I point on the page":

Look at me jump.

"Now think: What else could *you* say on this page? Use the snap word chart to help you. You can use other words, too." I gave a moment of think time. "Turn and tell your partner what else you could write."

I listened in. Some students said, "I can jump high" or "I like to jump." Others said sentences that were less patterned, such as, "My boots go up high."

Direct students' attention to the snap word chart. You might invite one or two kids to go up to the chart and manipulate the chart, creating sentences of their own.

I reconvened the class. "You came up with even *more!* You said we could write, 'I can jump high,' or 'I like to jump up and down.'" I chose a sentence to write that reflected the pattern we had started, and wrote it quickly, referring to the snap word chart and stretching out other words.

LINK

Remind students of their growth, and challenge them to use all they know to do more.

"Writers, when you came to school at the beginning of the year, you were drawing pictures, and then you put letters and labels on the page. And look at you now. Now you are writing sentences and lots of them! You *are* growing. Today, do the best you can to be a brave speller and a writer who writes more than one sentence! Remember to ask yourself, 'What else could I say on this page?' You can use the snap word chart or your snap word collection to help you write more sentences on every page."

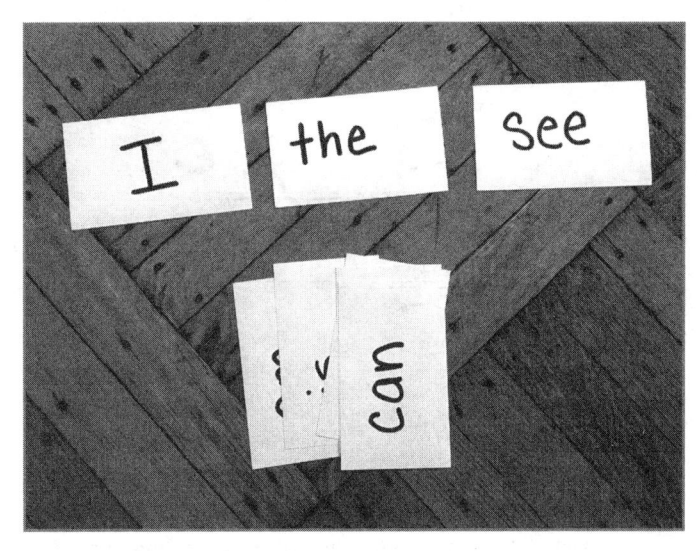

FIG. 16–1   A student lays out their snap word collection to make a sentence.

SESSION 16: WRITERS WRITE MORE SENTENCES ON A PAGE

CONFERRING AND SMALL-GROUP WORK

Supporting Phonics Transfer

PRIOR TO WRITING TODAY, you might take a few minutes to look across students' writing folders, studying their recent books with an eye for word study transfer. Note students who are regularly writing with beginning sounds and might be ready to include ending sounds in words. Look, also, for students who are writing with beginning and ending sounds and need support hearing medial sounds in words. Since this bend especially emphasizes work with high-frequency words, check that students are using these words regularly in their writing and that they are spelling them correctly. And of course, if you've taught other concepts during your phonics and word study time, you'll want to be on the lookout for those as well.

As you read students' writing, jot down the names of students who would benefit from small-group work around medial sounds and making patterns with high-frequency words. You can pull those groups during writing workshop, leading small groups that last five to seven minutes to support transference of these key phonics principles.

In a small group, support students who write with beginning and ending sounds to include medial sounds in words.

If you notice students who need help including medial sounds in words, you might begin a small group with a brief warm-up that helps students recall what they know about vowels. For instance, you could give copies of the vowel chart to partnerships and channel them to reread the chart, or engage them in singing "I like to eat, eat, eat apples and bananas."

Then, you might transition into a bit of targeted practice. You might say, "Writers, these letters you just read are so important—you'll find them in *every* word you write! Let's do a quiz. I'll say a word, then you write it down on the whiteboard, making sure that you have a vowel in your word. After you write the word, check to see if you have the same vowel as the person next to you." Select three words for kids to try, like *mat*, *fin*, and *let*. As kids are writing, encourage them to fix up their words to make the vowels they choose match the sounds from the vowel chart.

After this quick practice, invite students to remember to use vowels in their own writing. "Okay! Get going on your own piece. Remember that it is important that every word have a vowel. You can use the vowel chart to help you figure out the vowel that goes."

Coach children to incorporate this concept as they work:

- **If you see a word the child could add that would allow for short vowel practice:** "Try to add the word _____ to label your picture. Stretch out the word and use the vowel chart to help you. What vowel do you hear inside that word?"

- **If you see a word the child could try again to get the correct vowel sound:** "Try that word again. You forgot the vowel! Stretch it out and make sure

94

SHOW AND TELL WRITING: FROM LABELS TO PATTERN BOOKS

> **MID-WORKSHOP TEACHING**
> **Adding On When Your Words Don't Fit on the Page**
>
> "Writers, you're writing more and more sentences. Here's a tip. Often when you write more sentences, you need to write on more lines. When you get close to the end of the line, it is helpful to think, 'Can I fit this word here?' If it seems like it will be a tight squeeze, you can go to the beginning of the next line and start the word there." I held up a piece of writing paper and gestured to show this.
>
> "Or, you might realize you've written so much that you've run out of room on the page. If that happens, you could tape a revision strip onto the page." I held one up. "There's a basket of these in the writing center.
>
> "When you need a revision strip, grab one and use just two thumb-size pieces of tape to tape it on the bottom of your page, like this." I quickly demonstrated. "Otherwise, go back into your writing, and remember that when you hit the end of a line or the end of a page, you can keep writing more."

you hear the vowel." Place correction tape over the word or invite the child to cross it out and try again.

- **If a child is about to write a new word:** "Stretch it out and notice the vowel sound. What do you hear? What letter makes that sound?"

- **If you see a child writing a word with the correct vowel:** "You wrote the vowel ____. What sound did you hear?"

In a small group, support students with making patterns using snap words.

Some of your students might need more practice writing with snap words. If that's the case, you could convene a group where students practice making sentences for a booklet that only contains pictures.

Ask students to gather with their snap word baggies, filled with the high-frequency words they've learned during word study. "Writers, you know so many snap words. Right now, will you take them out of your baggie and reread them with your partner?" You might have just one student take their words out and use those for both members of the partnership.

Then, you might say, "These snap words can help you make sentences that you could write in books. Here are two books that don't have any sentences yet. These books need help!" Then, hand each partnership a booklet that contains just pictures—perhaps one with pictures of dogs and another with pictures of snacks. "Will you and your partner look at the pictures in these books and make sentences for each page using these snap words? You can make sentences like 'Here is . . . ' or 'Look at . . . ' Read each word as you put it in your sentence. Then, turn the page and try again with another picture!"

Once children have made a few sentences with their snap word cards, direct them to try this work with their own writing. "Writers, will you take out a book where you've drawn the pictures, but don't have the words on the line yet? Use the snap word cards to make sentences for your book. Try out a few to see which sentence you like the best." I coached children as they made sentences to go with their own writing with prompts like:

- "Remember to put the words from left to right. Put the first word here."

- "Is that a tricky word for you? That word is _____. Let's study it quickly."

- "Reread that sentence. Does it sound right? Let's make it sound right."

- "Try to look at a word and then write the whole word on the page. Then check it."

SHARE

Celebration

Introduce a song to celebrate the hard work students have done. Lead students in a shared reading and singing of the song.

"Writers, put your writing away and come to the rug quick! When people work hard, they celebrate. You all have been working hard! Your book factory has been making so many important books. Remind your partner about some of the books you've written already." I listened in as students talked, celebrating their range of topics.

"I've got a special song to help celebrate all your writing." I began to sing the song to the tune of Pharrell Williams's "Happy." I placed the lyrics on the easel, so kids could follow along. "Join me when you can!"

We sang the song a few times and then cheered to celebrate all students' hard work.

The Writing Song!

Sung to the tune of "Happy" by Pharrell Williams

Put your hands up if you wrote today
So much hard work, it's time to celebrate
We write good books and when we spell we're brave
Write the words we want to say and we fill the page

(Because I'm writing)
Clap along if you feel like you're a proud writer!
(Because I'm writing)
Clap along if you feel like you are now smarter!
(Because I'm writing)
Clap along if you know the things that writers do!
(Because I'm writing)
Clap along if you feel like you are proud of you!

96

SHOW AND TELL WRITING: FROM LABELS TO PATTERN BOOKS

Session 17

Writers Think about How Their Books Will End

IN THIS SESSION

TODAY YOU'LL teach writers that they can think about the endings of their books. You'll show a mentor text that ends with a big idea and then demonstrate how you draft an ending for the class book.

TODAY YOUR STUDENTS will return to books they have already drafted and add ending pages. Once they finish drafting endings for each of their books, they will start writing new books.

GETTING READY

- Before you teach, gather early reader books that end in different ways. We use *The Zoo* by Rose Lewis (Pioneer Valley Books), but you can use any favorite book in which the pattern changes and ends with a big idea (see Teaching and Mid-Workshop Teaching).

- Prior to the minilesson, place single sheets of blank paper on students' tables and in the writing center. Also put mini-staplers on each table (see Link).

- Have ready your class book on dancing so you can add an ending to it (see Teaching).

- Display and add a new point to the "Write a Show-and-Tell Book" anchor chart (see Link).

- Ask students to bring their writing folders to the rug (see Active Engagement).

MINILESSON

CONNECTION

Build excitement for the upcoming bookstore celebration at the end of the bend and unit. Compare the way people say goodbye to each other at the end of the day to the way authors end their books.

"Writers, we're getting closer to the bookstore celebration! I can't wait for you to share your books with the world—your classmates and other kids and maybe your family. You've got just two days to get your books ready for the bookstore! I thought of something that would make our books be bookstore-ready.

"You know how at the end of each school day, we say good-bye to each other? A lot of you give me a hug and say, 'See you tomorrow!' That's how we let each other know that the school day is over! Guess what? Authors do the same thing at the end of their books. They write a little ending that lets their reader know their book is over!"

❖ **Name the teaching point.**

"Writers, today I want to teach you that endings of books matter. Writers think carefully about how the last pages of their books could go. They make sure every book they write has an ending."

TEACHING

Emphasize how most of the book follows the same pattern, and then highlight how the author ends the book by naming a big idea.

"To figure out how writers write their endings, let's study a book called *The Zoo*. I'll read, and will you pay attention to how the author ends this book?"

I read aloud, pausing before the last page. "Okay, so far each page has told about a different animal at the zoo: the tigers, the giraffes, the elephants, the monkeys. I wonder what animal will be on the last page."

I turned and read the last page.

We like going to the zoo!

"Wait a second! This last page is different. It broke the pattern. The other pages all told about the animals in the zoo, but this page says that the kids like going to the zoo. It's almost like the ending tells a big idea about the whole book."

Channel children to think with you as you consider and write an ending with a demonstration text.

"I bet we could end our books the same way! We could end with a big idea. Let's look at our book about dancing. I wonder how this book could end.

"I'll reread what we have so far, and will you think about a big idea we could end with?" I read the pages aloud.

"Could we end with a big idea about dancing? How could the ending sound? Turn and talk with your partner." I listened in to see if kids were starting to get the idea. "I agree! This book could end with: 'I love dancing' or 'Dancing is fun.'"

I grabbed a new piece of paper and stapled it to the back of the book. Then I quickly drew a kid with a big smile. I added and said the words, "Dancing is fun."

"Writers, do you see how we thought hard about how the book could end and wrote a page that told a big idea about our topic?"

ACTIVE ENGAGEMENT

Invite children to reread one of their books and think about how the next page could go. After they read and think, ask them to share their ending with a partner.

"Give it a try right now. Pull one of your books out of your writing folder. Reread your book and think about how it could end. What's a big idea you have about your topic?" I listened as students reread their books.

Soon your students will be reading level B books. A characteristic of level B is that the pattern changes at the end. This is an introduction to level B books.

You could replace this book with any book that has an ending where the pattern changes and reflects the big idea of the book. Most level B books have a pattern change similar to this at the end.

"Now share your ending with a partner. What will your ending page say?" I coached students.

After children shared with one another, I shared out one idea. "Logan said his ending page will say, 'Basketball is super!' Your readers will love these thoughtful endings you're writing."

LINK

Encourage students to write endings for each of their books. Explain how they can use tools to add new pages to their books.

"Writers, when you go off today, instead of writing new books, will you first make endings for all of your books?" I added a new Post-it, "Write more! Write an ending" to the anchor chart, "To Write a Show-and-Tell Book."

ANCHOR CHART

To Write a Show-and-Tell Book
- Think of an idea.
- Tell all the parts.
- Draw and write the parts.
- Write more! Bring pages to life.
- Write more! Write sentences.
- **Write more! Write an ending.**

"You might be thinking, 'I need paper!' I've placed some blank pages on your table and in the writing center so that you can write ending pages for your books. I've also placed some mini-staplers on your tables so that you can staple your ending to the end of your book after you write it. Let me show you how to do this carefully."

I quickly showed students how to add a page by stapling it in one corner. "After you finish writing an ending for one book, you'll pick up another book and write the ending. If you finish writing endings for all of your books, the writing center will be open so that you can start a new one. Off you go, writers. Let's have another great day in the book factory!"

CONFERRING AND SMALL-GROUP WORK

Support Early Revision Habits

FOR THE YOUNGEST WRITERS, editing and revision often seem like the same thing, even though they're not. When we think of editing, we think of kids going back and adding in punctuation, fixing snap words, or adding capitals at the beginning of sentences. In contrast, revision at these early stages might be going back and adding more details or labels to their pictures, adding another sentence to their page, or adding a new page. Because of that, revision work is a challenging skill for students to learn, and practicing it early is key.

In a small group, help students revise their books by adding more to existing pages or adding new pages.

You'll have some students who finish books quickly and immediately move on to the next. You could call these writers together and conduct a small group that helps them return to books to revise. As in all of your small groups, you'll begin by naming the reason why you've called students together.

"One challenge writers sometimes have is finding ways to make their finished work better. When writers return to books that are almost done, they have choices. They can go back and add more to their pages. And they can add more pages to their books, too! When you return to a book, you can ask, 'What else can I say? Should I add it onto a page I already have? Or add it onto a new page because it is a new part?'

"Take a look at one of your finished books. Reread your book. Think, 'Could I add more on a page, or could I add a new page to tell something else?'"

As students reread and get started, you can coach in with prompts like:

- "What else could you say/draw/label in this part?"
- "Look at the page and think about what you could add."
- "Let's look back at your parts. What else could you write about in your book? Get a new page!"

You can close the group by reminding writers that they can do this in all their books, and that the writing center has pages to add to their books anytime.

MID-WORKSHOP TEACHING
Making Endings Exciting with Exclamation Points

"Writers, let me show you something else about the pages and sentences in some books. Sometimes you want the ending of your book to sound a little exciting. To do this, you can use a special mark at the end of the sentence—called an *exclamation point*." I held up the ending page of the book we studied in the minilesson that had an exclamation point, and then I walked quickly from table to table to show it off.

"It says, 'We like going to the zoo!' and then there's that mark here: an exclamation point. We can say it in an excited voice. Let's say it together in excited voices." The class joined me as we read. "If you want a sentence or your book ending to sound excited, you could use an exclamation point, too! I'll draw one here on the easel, so you can see what it looks like."

SHARE

Sharing Endings with a Symphony Share

Channel writers to celebrate and share their endings by reading their ending pages aloud as you point to them. Then, invite the class to read their endings all at once.

"Writers, find a book ending that you wrote today and open up to it. In just a minute, you're going to read the ending page of your book aloud, for us all to hear. But first, practice pointing and reading your ending in a whisper voice." I gave students a moment to find the page and rehearse.

"When I point to you with my magic writing wand, will you read your ending loud and proud?" I pointed to five or six students and they read their endings. "Now, will you all read your endings at the same time? Are you ready? One, two, three, go!" Students read their endings aloud.

"What a beautiful symphony of book endings. Bravo, writers!"

Session 18

Fancying Up Your Writing

GETTING READY

- Before you teach, prepare a page of your class book so it has some editing mistakes—a lowercase letter at the beginning of a sentence, a misspelled snap word, or a missing word (see Teaching and Active Engagement).
- Students need to bring their writing folders to the rug (see Link).
- Prepare a "ready for the bookstore" bin to hold children's completed books (see Link).
- Display the "To Write a Show-and-Tell Book" anchor chart and the "Snap Words You May Know (including More Snap Words)" chart. Be ready to put stars on those charts and the sentence (see Teaching and Active Engagement and Conferring and Small-Group Work).
- Bring empty baskets to the rug (see Share).

IN THIS SESSION

TODAY YOU'LL teach writers that they can prepare their writing for an audience by making sure their sentences look like a book, adding more sentences, and ensuring that each book has an ending. You'll work with the class to check for these things in the class book before sending children off to try it with their own books.

TODAY YOUR STUDENTS will select and prepare books for publication. Expect to see students fixing up spelling and capitalization, adding sentences, and adding pages for endings.

MINILESSON

CONNECTION

Remind students of the upcoming celebration: a bookstore. Explain that when writers get ready to share their writing with the world, they take time to make their stories beautiful.

"This is a really important day in our book factory. You've worked so hard to make books that kids want to read. But you haven't stopped there! You've also learned lots of ways to write books—to be brave spellers, to come up with ideas, to write across pages, and to write sentences. Before you get ready to share your pieces at the bookstore, there's still some important work left to do.

"When writers get ready to show their writing with the world, they take time to make their stories beautiful. Writers want people to look at their book and say, 'I've got to pick this one up and look at it. I've got to turn the pages.'"

❖ **Name the teaching point.**

"Today I want to teach you that before writers share their books with the world, they spend time making their writing the best it can be. To do this, you can reread and make sure your sentences look like a book, that you have lots of sentences on each page, and finally, that your books have endings. If something is missing, you can add it in or revise it!"

TEACHING AND ACTIVE ENGAGEMENT

Use the charts from the unit to remind students how to fix up their writing. Then, recruit them to help you revise the book to make it ready to share with the world.

"Let's make our class book about dancing bookstore-ready. As we look at the pages and read the words, be thinking about which of these three things we could do to make our writing beautiful and ready for the shelves—making sentences look like a book, adding sentences, or making sure we have endings. We've got charts to help us remember this. I've starred the parts of our charts that are especially important." I gestured toward our anchor chart, "To Write a Show-and-Tell Book," where I'd placed stars next to the final two points, "Write more! Write sentences" and "Write more! Write an ending." I also starred the snap word chart.

I gestured for students to read the book along with me. We checked the first two pages to make sure that the sentences looked right and that there was more than one sentence on the page. We got to the third page, which read:

look ta me twist.

"Okay, let's check this page. Does this sentence look like a book? Does it have lots of sentences? Talk with your partner."

After children discussed the sentence, I called them back together. "I heard Jason saying that he thinks we should fix up the snap word *at*. Jason, come on up. Write the word *at* just like it looks on the snap word chart. Everyone else, let's say it and write the word *at* in the air."

"The first letter should be big, too," said Selena.

"You're right. Selena, come and fix up this sentence so it has an uppercase letter at the beginning of the word *Look*."

"Anything else?" I reread the page.

"Add more!" children said, noticing that there was only one sentence. "Yes! We can add lots of sentences! What could we add? Turn and talk."

When writers have an authentic purposes for writing, they are much more likely to do their best work. We want to create opportunities for students to share their books with the world. You might put them in the school library after the bookstore to continue the celebration.

SESSION 18: FANCYING UP YOUR WRITING   **103**

I listened to children for a minute and said, "I'll add this one." I wrote:

I can twist back and forth.

"Okay, we checked to make sure our sentences look like a book and we checked for lots of sentences. Next, let's check for an ending." I read the next page. "Oh yes, this book has an ending. Some of your books won't. If they don't, add one!"

LINK

Ask children to reread one book they've written, considering what they need to do to fancy it up. Then, send them off to fancy up several books during writing time. Invite writers to put finished books in a "ready for the bookstore" basket.

"Writers, you've got a big job today. You'll need to publish and fancy up as many books as you can, to put them on display at tomorrow's bookstore. To start, will you pull out one book from your folder? Reread it and think, 'What do I need to do to fancy this book up, to make it ready to share with the world?' Do you need to add sentences? Do you need to add an ending?"

I gave students a minute to reread their book. "Tell your partner what you'll do to make this first book ready for the world to read.

"Head back and get started! When you finish fancying that one up, put it in the 'ready for the bookstore' bin I've placed up here. We'll need to have lots of fancied-up books for tomorrow's bookstore! Off you go!"

As students are finishing up their books, you will want to balance accepting students' approximations with holding them accountable for work you've taught in this unit. In deciding when to send someone back to keep working, use your knowledge of that student's zone of proximal development.

CONFERRING AND SMALL-GROUP WORK

Celebrate Process over Product

AS YOU PREPARE YOUR STUDENTS for the celebration, keep in mind that your goal is to highlight the effort your students have put forth, not the product they've produced. As Ralph Waldo Emerson said, "Life is a journey, not a destination." As you come to the end of this unit, celebrate the growth and bravery your students demonstrated, not just the pieces of writing they produced.

In the scores of classrooms that do this work, we have found that kindergarten writers do not benefit from copying and rewriting books. Kids this age usually see recopying as writing a new book, and they tend to make new mistakes or recopy the same mistakes. It also communicates to kids that the books they've worked so hard on are not good enough to display and celebrate. That's the last thing we want kids to think. You want them to be proud of all the changes they've made.

Voiceovers that Encourage Kids to Do Their Best Work

Fixing up snap words:

- "Get your snap word collection out. Match up the snap words from the baggie with the ones on your page. Did you get every letter? Do you have to change any letters?"

Making sentences look like a book:

- "Reread your sentences and take a close look. Remember how sentences start and end. Make sure that you start with an uppercase letter, use mostly lowercase letters throughout, and end with punctuation. If you didn't, fix it up! Use the sentence up on the chart to help you remember."

Adding more sentences to pages:

- "Reread your sentence. Try to add another one on this page. What else could you say? Use your snap words to help you."

Writing endings:

- "If you need to add an ending, reread your whole book. Then think: How could this book end? What's a big idea I have about this topic? Perhaps it is what *you* think. Then, add a page and write your ending down!"

MID-WORKSHOP TEACHING
Fancying Up One Book and Then Another

"Writers, you've worked so hard to make your writing ready to share with the world at tomorrow's bookstore! Guess what? Once you finish fancying up one book, your work is not done. You can choose another book to fancy up!

"Right now, choose the next book you are going to make beautiful. Hold it up!" I waited until students were holding up another book they were going to publish. "Awesome! Get started! Look at the charts for things that you can fix."

SESSION 18: FANCYING UP YOUR WRITING

SHARE

Sorting Books to Get Ready for the Bookstore

Coach students to sort books into categories that they will display for tomorrow's bookstore.

"Writers, come quickly to the meeting area. Our bookstore opens tomorrow! One thing that bookstores have is different places for different kinds of books. I thought we could put our books together in groups or categories, that way people would know what they were looking for. I have these baskets for us to separate the books into.

"We could put all the robot books together, or we could put all the imaginary books in one basket and all the real stuff books into another basket. It's up to you. Let's lay all our books out on the rug so we can see how they might go together. First we're going to look and talk then we'll decide where they go."

I gave students a few minutes to lay all their books out on the carpet, and then talk about where they might go. Once students had decided on some categories, I brought them back together.

"Now we can make some labels for these baskets, so everyone knows what kind of books are in there." I handed out sentence strips and sent students off to their tables to make labels for the different book bins. They made labels like "Robot books," "Mermaid books," "Scary things," and "Grandmas."

Session 19

Bookstore Celebration

Dear Teachers,

Today is the day! It's time to celebrate the brave effort your students put forth during this unit. What better way to do this than by creating a bookstore that lets students play *and* put all the books they've created on display for the public? In this unit, we choose to depart from a normal writing celebration to tap into the enormous imaginations of kindergartners. Play is an essential part of any primary classroom, and unfortunately, it's something that is disappearing. While playing, students engage in deep conversations, learn self-reliance, engage in problem solving, and grapple with how to be part of a larger community. The idea for this bookstore celebration came from our love of independent bookstores. Independent bookstores are absolutely a representation of what a community holds dear. They are gathering places that celebrate literacy, where one might go for a workshop, an author reading, or to listen to a read-aloud of a new children's book. Creating a homegrown bookstore could be the perfect way to celebrate a unit that asks students to make books that represent who they are. Here, we offer suggestions for how the bookstore might go, but ultimately it should be a reflection of your unique classroom community.

If the idea of a bookstore seems daunting, you could do a tried and true celebration from earlier in the unit. Instead of inviting parents, you could invite fifth-graders or other students into the room to celebrate student's work. Your students could sit at their desks and talk about their books to an invited guest or two, receiving praise (see Session 11 share). Or you could invite another class in and invite students take part in a museum share where they walk around looking at each other's work and putting comments on it (see Session 5 share). You might simply ask students to reflect on their growth by taking out the time capsule of their old work and comparing the old to the new. All of these options would be a perfect culmination.

If you decide to go ahead with the bookstore celebration, the logistics will be important. You'll need a period to get ready for the bookstore and another period to hold the bookstore, perhaps during your dramatic play time. You'll also need to invite an audience in to read, listen, or shop. And, if possible, you'll need another adult or two to help with classroom management as students make materials for the bookstore and while they celebrate in different parts of the classroom.

To get your classroom "bookstore ready," instead of holding a regular writing workshop, we suggest that you spend some time today brainstorming with students on how to turn the classroom into a bookstore. You might gather your students on the rug and say, "Writers, today we are opening our bookstore! Your friends and families are going to come by later to see all your hard work! The best part of all the work you've done is that you've not just made a lot of books, but you've made books that are *important* to you. Books that you believe should exist in the world. To show off all this important work I thought we could take some time to make our classroom look like a bookstore. You're great at thinking about the parts of things, so will you and your partner talk about what parts make up a bookstore?" If kids can't come up with ideas, you might show a few photos of bookstores from printed or online sources to help spark discussion.

After a minute, you might say, "Wow! Bookstores have lots of parts. Let's list all those jobs on a chart, and then we can divide up who will work on each job."

Possible jobs for students might be:

- Creating a café for the room: making pretend coffee cups, baked goods, a menu, and more.
- Making a cash register, play money, and price tags for the books.
- Staging a read-aloud area: making a hat for the person reading, drafting a sign for the read-aloud space.
- Designing signs for the hallway to invite people to the bookstore.

Once you are ready to open the bookstore, gather your students on the rug, and invite the visitors into the room. You might say something like "Visitors, over the course of this unit, we realized that our classroom didn't have books that showed who we are or what we like . . . so we decided to make books about those things. We turned our classroom into a book factory! There are now books in this classroom about fairies, Legos, little brothers, Pokémon cards, and so much more. We thought we should share our books with the world, because maybe other people would want to read about the things we wrote about. So today we are going to have a bookstore." Then lead students in chant from one of their old favorites, *Caps for Sale*, but instead of *caps*, students could say "Books, Books, for sale! Fifty cents a book!" We're not expecting that people actually pay your students for their books, you might want to make sure students and adults know you are playing pretend.

You'll send students off to their spots and then send the adults off to admire the work students have done. You could encourage adults to ask students to read their books to them, or to ask them to sign their books for them on an autograph page. You'll want to remind students about how to talk about their work, saying what they are proud of, and you might bring back the Session 11 chart, "Writers Talk About Their Writing."

When it is time to bring the celebration to an end, close the bookstore by gathering students together to reflect on the growth they've made over the course of this unit. You might even bring back your time capsule of their work from the first day of writing workshop (see Session 5). You could say, "Writers, we are all so blown away by how much you've grown as writers. Remember how you looked at your writing from the beginning of the year, earlier in this unit? I have it here again, and I'm going to pass it out. As I do, will you look at how much you've grown as a writer. Turn and tell your partner what you are proud of. You might use the words, 'I used to . . . and now. . . .'"

Ultimately, this is your chance to celebrate that students are now people who see themselves as writers, who are using pictures and words to communicate about who they are. You might say something like "You are now the kind of writers like Joy Cowley and Mo Willems, writers who write about things that are important to them and share those books with the world. This is what we are going to be doing for the rest of the year and hopefully you'll do this for the rest of your lives." Celebrate by singing your newest anthem, "The Writing Song!," from Session 16.

All the best,
Marie and Lizzie